TOM PETTY

Tom Petty, at the time of his commercial breakthrough in the 1970s.

TOM PETTY THE LIFE & MUSIC

Gillian G. Gaar

Tom in 1986, awaiting inspiration in Mike Campbell's garage studio.

CONTENTS

INTRODUCTION

Tom Petty wore his fame lightly. He even professed that his music wasn't all that important, dismissing his songs as "cheap shit, disposable crap," in the pages of *Rolling Stone*. When the magazine called him out on his comments the following year, he was quick to clarify his remarks: "I didn't mean it's cheap shit—what we've done means an awful lot to me. But I can't approach it seriously. I can't sit down and say, 'Here's a classic.' I've got to say it's disposable. You move on to the next thing; you can't dwell on what you've done. But if the old ones live forever, great."

Of course, the truth of the matter is that Tom did take his music seriously—the writing of it, the recording of it, and the performing of it. And he did manage to come up with some classics along the way: "Free Fallin'," "Refugee," "Don't Come Around Here No More," "I Won't Back Down," and, of course, "American Girl," to mention just a few. And not a disposable one in the bunch.

Music had been the driving force in his life, since meeting Elvis Presley at the age of ten, and acquiring a box of rock 'n' roll 45s soon after. He loved the stuff, couldn't get enough of it. It's what made his radio show, *Tom Petty's Buried Treasure,* such a delight to listen to. He loved turning people on to good music—and it didn't have to be his own. "The feedback I get is so rewarding," he told *Parade* magazine. "I get such nice mail: people remembering things or discovering things. A teenage girl wrote me saying she'd never heard of Chuck Berry. I couldn't believe it. It's so rewarding to be passing that music on to people."

It was the music business that caused Tom more aggravation. And he had no problem standing up for himself if he felt he was being taken advantage of. He was willing to declare bankruptcy to get out of what he considered to be an unfair contract. And he didn't hesitate to fight with his record label again when he was informed the company would be charging an extra dollar for his latest album. He was especially proud to have won that battle, noting that album prices didn't rise for a number of years after his complaints.

Dealing with the music business was a necessary evil. But Tom was smart enough to not let it detract from the more important business of making music. He enjoyed the camaraderie of being in a band; despite his group billed as "Tom Petty and the Heartbreakers," he had no wish to be seen as fronting a band of anonymous session musicians who changed every tour. "I never saw another band where I went, 'Wow, I wish I could be in that band,'" he told journalist David Fricke. "I always thought I was in the best band. And I still feel that way." Tom wanted the interaction that comes from working with people over an extended period, creating something that's bigger than yourself.

His sudden death in 2017 was especially tragic because at just sixty-six years old, Tom seemed far too young to have his voice silenced. As he reflected on his career in 2014, he noted there was still a lot he wanted to do and that he was proud of what had been accomplished so far: "Music I made in the Seventies—I still hear it on the radio. It's the mark I left in the world while I was here. I have some great shows people will remember, but that's the real work in me: the records."

Tom Petty's music left a pretty good sized mark in the world. And there was something else about him that he never wanted the world to forget. As described by *Rolling Stone*, "Tom Petty can only think of one epitaph for himself, he says, just one phrase to tell people who he was: HE REALLY LIKED ROCK & ROLL."

Tom at what was then London's Hammersmith Odeon (today the Eventim Apollo). Tom experienced his first commercial success in the UK.

PART 1

RUNNIN' DOWN A DREAM, 1950–1979

A young Tom Petty, preparing to take on the music world.

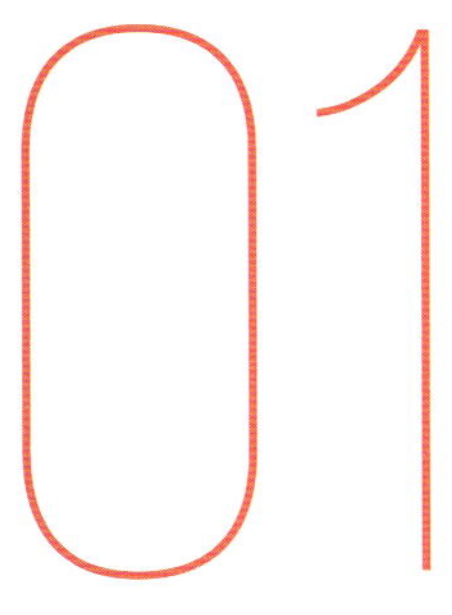

THE JOURNEY BEGINS

Tom managed to pose for his school yearbook photo, even though school wasn't his favorite place to be.

TOM PETTY MAKES HIS ENTRANCE

OCTOBER 20, 1950

Earl Petty was born into a working-class family of laborers in Argyle, Georgia, in 1924. When he was six years old, the family moved to Reddick, Florida, where the hard life continued. Earl left his hometown for good when he served in the US Air Force during World War II, and he settled in Gainesville, about 24 miles (39 km) north of Reddick, when he was discharged. He became a truck driver for Eli Witt's Candy and Tobacco store, where he met Katherine Avery (born in 1927), who worked in the office. Like Earl, Katherine's family had originally come from Georgia. The two married in 1947. Three years later, Thomas Earl Petty was born. A second son, Bruce, was born in 1958.

The family lived in a two-bedroom ranch-style house near a park. On the surface, the Pettys appeared to be just another ordinary, happy family. But in reality, Tom Petty's childhood was more like a tale of Southern Gothic horror. His father worked as a salesman of dry goods, then sold insurance. Maybe the fact that he never landed that big sale fueled a darkness within him. Earl became an alcoholic. That was followed by physical violence, with Earl beating Tom so badly he left welts on his son's body. It was also a family of secrets. Earl was actually of mixed race, born to a Caucasian father and a Native American Cherokee mother. It was a subject the family never spoke about, though it was rumored that this was the real reason they'd left Georgia. Tom's mother falling ill with cancer was another hardship for the family to deal with (Katherine Petty died in 1980 at age fifty-three, a day after Tom's thirtieth birthday).

As Tom grew up, conflicts with his father increased; there always seemed to be something that disappointed Earl. Tom didn't like sports. He had no interest in those good ol' boy activities of hunting and fishing. He was a failure at school—not due to his lack of intelligence, but a lack of interest in his studies (though as a keen reader, he did well in English). And then there was his hair, which was definitely too long. Tom later mused that his father may have worried that his son's long hair meant he was gay. But the real reason Tom never brought any girlfriends home was because he was reluctant to bring anybody, let alone someone he wanted to impress, into such a dysfunctional household.

So from a young age, Tom Petty dreamed of escape. And the family's television set provided a portal into another world. When an announcer would state that a program was being broadcast from "Television City in Hollywood," it sounded like a magical destination. "I thought, 'Television City? Man, that's where I need to be,'" he later told his biographer. He also noted that a number of the shows he watched came from California. He'd begun to feel the lure of the West, and by his mid-twenties he would turn his California dreaming into reality.

There were some bright spots. Tom and his brother spent hours watching westerns on TV, then played at being cowboys in the backyard. Neighborhood kids would come over to play in the partially completed bomb shelter Earl had built in the backyard, in preparation for a foreign invasion or nuclear attack. Tom had friends at school too, though as he grew older actually attending class became less of a priority.

If nothing else, his parents' example showed him what he *didn't* want to do with his life. He sure didn't want to waste it in the drudgery of sales or office work. And he'd soon find the inspiration to help him take the next step. As he jokingly explained when he later received the George and Ira Gershwin Award for Lifetime Achievement, "I started listening to music when I was a very young kid, like eleven years old—and my life has basically gone to hell ever since."

Go West, Young Man: California, the Golden State, was seen as a land of opportunity, especially for those in the entertainment industry.

"THE SOUNDTRACK OF MY EARLY YEARS"

At age ten, Tom was just one of millions of Elvis Presley fans in the United States. But unlike most of those fans, he actually met his idol.

A KING-SIZE ENCOUNTER

SUMMER 1961

Presley's skyrocketing success in the 1950s was put on hold by his two-year army hitch, from 1958 to 1960. And until he became lost in Hollywood mediocrity, the 1960s started out well for him, with hit songs and albums such as "It's Now or Never" and *Elvis Is Back!*, and the equally successful films *G.I. Blues* and *Blue Hawaii*. In July 1961, Presley arrived in Crystal River, Florida, on the western coast of the state, for location shooting of his ninth film, *Follow That Dream*.

Tom's uncle, Earl Jernigan, ran a film developing business in Florida, and he earned money on the side working on local film shoots. When he signed on to work on *Follow That Dream*, ten-year-old Tom was asked if he'd like to come to the film set and meet Elvis. Tom agreed, more because it was something to do than that he was excited about meeting Presley; he knew Elvis was a rock star, but "I'd never thought much about rock 'n' roll until that moment."

That was destined to change. Jernigan's wife, Evelyn, picked up Tom and two of his cousins and drove them to the nearby town of Ocala, where a scene was being shot of Elvis and his costar Anne Helm walking into a bank. Tom was amazed at the crowds waiting for a glimpse of the King, the anticipation building as a fleet of white Cadillacs appeared, carrying Elvis' entourage. Finally, Elvis himself got out of a Caddy. "He stepped out, radiant as an angel," Petty later recalled. "He seemed to glow and walk above the ground. It was like nothing I'd ever seen in my life."

Uncle Earl introduced the children to Elvis, who smiled and greeted them. "I don't know what he said, because I was just too dumbfounded," Tom later recalled. He was equally astonished by the crowd's reaction throughout the day. Each time Elvis pulled up in his car during the scene,

Elvis Presley in the 1962 film *Follow That Dream*. During location shooting in Florida, a young Tom was able to meet the King of Rock 'n' Roll.

a few fans would somehow get past the barricade, meaning a simple scene took that much longer to shoot. He also noted with envy the fans waving album covers that members of Elvis' entourage would take to the dressing room to have signed; why hadn't *he* thought of bringing a record cover for an autograph? The day was about more than just meeting a rock star. It was about witnessing, first-hand, the power of stardom, which left him thinking, "That is one hell of a job to have."

When Tom arrived back home, his neighbor Keith Harben was waiting for him, eager to hear every detail. He could tell that his friend had been deeply affected by the experience. "It was like a switch turned on for him," Harben later told reporter Noel Leroux. "It turned the light on in his head. It was just a magical moment for Tom." Harben had a collection of Elvis 45s that his older sister had given him, and Petty quickly arranged to trade his Wham-O slingshot for them. He'd become a student of rock 'n' roll.

It wasn't surprising that Presley's songs later found their way into Petty's live performances. In 2011, he listed the Elvis songs that most influenced him for *Rolling Stone*: "That's All Right," "Baby Let's Play House," "Heartbreak Hotel," "Hound Dog," "Mean Woman Blues," "One Night with You," "Santa Claus Is Back in Town," "Can't Help Falling in Love," "A Mess of Blues," and "(Marie's the Name) His Latest Flame." Tom was also one of the interviewees in the Presley documentary *The Searcher* (2018)—still a loyal subject of the King.

"IT WAS ELECTRIFYING"

THE BEATLES ON *ED SULLIVAN*

FEBRUARY 9, 1964

As Tom was walking around his neighborhood one Sunday in February, another boy passing by on his bicycle called out to him, "Hey, the Beatles are on TV tonight." What made the moment especially significant was that the two didn't even know each other, but the boy still thought that news of the Beatles' arrival was so important he had to pass it along to someone. "I thought to myself, 'This means something,'" Tom later told *Guitar World*.

After releasing their first record in 1962, the Beatles had taken their native Britain by storm in 1963, with a string of chart-topping albums and singles. US success took longer to arrive; the band's US label, Capitol, initially dumped the band's singles off on smaller independent labels, where they sank without a trace. But things turned around when Capitol released "I Want to Hold Your Hand" in December 1963. The single took off and quickly topped the charts, handily promoting the band's upcoming appearances on *The Ed Sullivan Show* in February.

Tom probably didn't need a reminder that the Beatles were going to be on *Ed Sullivan*. He was already a fan and had insisted that his school friend Keith Harben accompany him to a dance held at the Gainesville Recreation Center to hear their latest records being played. But that was nothing compared to seeing them perform. "You just knew it, sitting in your living room, that everything around you was changing," Tom observed. "It was like going from black-and-white to color."

Sullivan opened the show by having the Beatles perform three songs, then come on again later in the program to perform two more. Tom recalled the agony of that wait, having to sit through magician Fred Kaps, comedian Frank Gorshin, and others before the Fab Four finally returned to sing "I Want to Hold Your Hand" (another act performing that night was the cast of the musical *Oliver!*, featuring future Monkee Davy Jones among them). Tom was fascinated by the studio audience's reaction, similar to the excitement he'd seen Elvis generate among the crowds watching him while filming *Follow That Dream*. And it was exciting to hear that next week's show, also featuring the Beatles, would be broadcast from Tom's own home state—at the Deauville Hotel in Miami, Florida.

Tom was immediately fired up, studying the music on the band's album *Meet the Beatles!* with the same careful attention he'd devoted to listening to his Elvis 45s. He also saw how the Beatles' influence had quickly spread through Gainesville's burgeoning music scene. When he next caught a local band called the Escorts, who featured Duane and Gregg Allman in their lineup, he was impressed by their Beatles-styled collarless jackets and their long hair. And every up-and-coming band seemed to include a Beatles song in their setlist.

Petty was no different. He already had a guitar, a Stella acoustic he acquired in 1962. But that wasn't what the Beatles were playing, and he soon managed to scrape up the twenty-five dollars necessary to pay for a Kay electric guitar, taking lessons at Lipham Music, a store in the Gainesville Shopping Plaza (Don Felder, fellow Gainesville resident and future Eagles guitarist, wrote in his memoir that he gave Tom a few lessons, but Petty himself recalled that Felder gave him piano lessons). At the same time, up in Jacksonville, future Heartbreakers guitarist Mike Campbell, similarly inspired, got his hands on a guitar and began practicing on it "from the time I came home from school until I went to bed."

It was a life-changing moment that set the course for Petty's career. As Tom said to *Billboard*, once he saw the Beatles on *Ed Sullivan,* "I knew exactly what I wanted to do with my life, no question."

The Beatles' appearances on *The Ed Sullivan Show* provided inspiration to millions of budding musicians across the US—including Tom Petty. Here the band stands by prior to their second appearance on the program, filmed February 16, 1964, at the Deauville Hotel in Miami Beach, Florida.

TOM'S FIRST SINGLE

"UP IN MISSISSIPPI"/ "CAUSE IS UNDERSTOOD"

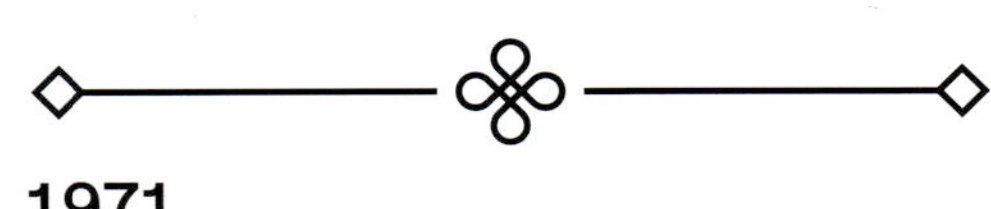

1971

Tom's first record came in 1971 with his Florida band, Mudcrutch. A few years later he and the band were sitting for promo photo shoots.

Tom formed his first band at age fourteen to impress a girl. A fellow classmate, Cindy, had mentioned how much she liked a certain song on the radio (Tom thought it might have been by British Invasion act Wayne Fontana and the Mindbenders), and he boasted that his band could play it. Cindy immediately agreed to have the band play at the next school dance. The only problem: Tom didn't actually have a band.

But he managed to rustle one up by the time of the dance, asking other school friends to join a combo that was called the Sundowners. The group, with Tom on bass, played cover songs of current hits (especially by British Invasion acts), at teenage venues like schools and community centers, and eventually fraternities. Tom left the band after a fight with the drummer, but he was quickly asked to join another local band, the Epics.

The Epics, most of whose members were older than Tom, were a step above the teen circuit the Sundowners played. Tom stayed with the group until 1969, when he left for Tampa where he was briefly enrolled in art college. But he soon returned to Gainesville and rejoined the band.

By then, the Epics were transitioning into a new group, Mudcrutch. This led to various lineup changes; at one point, the band was down to a trio, following the departure of Rick and Rodney Rucker, who'd founded the Epics. Tom (on bass), Jim Lenahan (vocals), and Tom Leadon (guitar) eventually found a drummer, Randall Marsh, whose roommate, Mike Campbell, also joined the band on guitar.

Marsh and Campbell lived outside Gainesville in a house soon rechristened "Mudcrutch Farm." It quickly became a party house for local musicians; they even held a regular "Mudcrutch Farm Festival" until too many neighbors complained. Lenahan was eased out of the group, with Petty taking over on lead vocals.

The group worked to stand out from other local bands by performing original material. The next step? Making a record. Gerald Maddox, a friend of Marsh's, offered to put up money for a recording session. Mudcrutch booked time at Criteria Studios in Miami, where numerous legendary artists had recorded, including James Brown ("I Got You [I Feel Good]"), Aretha Franklin (*Young, Gifted and Black*), and Eric Clapton (*Layla and Other Assorted Love Songs*). Leadon's brother Bernie, who had moved to California and soon became a member of the Eagles, gave them tips on how to work in the studio. They stayed in a nearby motel the night before the session, everyone too nervous to sleep.

The next day they recorded two of Tom's songs. The upbeat country rock "Up in Mississippi" belies its underlying sadness, as Petty sings about losing his "old girl" to a wealthier man in the big city (Biloxi). "Cause Is Understood" is a harder rocking number, culminating in a frantic guitar solo. Not a bad effort for a first release.

The band pressed 500 copies of the single. As Maddox's family ran a pepper farm, they decided to call their label Pepper Records (Gerry Maddox was also credited as executive producer). The single received enough local airplay that it reached #1 at radio station WGGG. But that was as far as it went. The record pushed the band's profile up a notch, but it ended up not being much of a stepping stone. It was time to push further afield. Petty now had his eyes set on two goals: "to make records and sell them, to play shows in places other than Florida."

Most of the singles ended up in Tom Leadon's closet, where he left them behind when he moved. It was the first Tom Petty–related collectible, and at the time of writing, a copy of the single was worth a minimum of $1,400.

THE RECORD DEAL

Mudcrutch was the band that finally got Tom out of Florida. The indoor shot shows, from left, Mike Campbell, Petty, Tom Leadon, and Randall Marsh. Mudcrutch's 1975 single, "Depot Street," got some good notices, but failed to make an impact on the charts.

MUDCRUTCH SIGNS WITH SHELTER RECORDS

SPRING 1974

Mudcrutch was in a rut. And Tom felt he had the answer: go west.

Tom Leadon had been kicked out of the band following an argument with a club owner. He was replaced by multi-instrumentalist Danny Roberts, who shared lead vocals with Petty. Mudcrutch had also taken on a keyboardist, Benmont Tench. The new lineup recorded a demo tape of original songs, which was sent out to record companies. When it got a nibble of interest from LA-based Playboy Records, Tom decided to head for California.

He took Danny and Mudcrutch roadie Keith McAllister along for the drive. Playboy ultimately turned them down, but there were plenty of other labels in town to hit up. It was decided to go with London Records (who released the Rolling Stones' records in the US), who offered them an album deal. So everyone headed back to Gainesville to bring the full band to LA. But before the return trip to the West Coast, a call came in from Denny Cordell, from LA label Shelter Records. He'd also heard the demo and wanted Mudcrutch to sign with him.

Cordell, born in Argentina, had worked for Island Records and had also produced such acts as the Moody Blues, Joe Cocker, and Procol Harum's "Whiter Shade of Pale" single. He had started Shelter Records with musician Leon Russell; they also owned two studios in Tulsa, Oklahoma. It was an impressive resume, and

Mudcrutch agreed to drive to Tulsa to meet Cordell in person. While there, they also recorded a few demos at the label's Church Studio. Cordell promptly fronted the band some money and sent everyone on to LA to sign a formal contract.

The band first lived in a hotel near Shelter's offices on Hollywood Boulevard, then moved to two houses in the San Fernando Valley. When they were finally deemed ready to record, Cordell set them up at Village Recorders studio. At his suggestion, the song he'd earmarked for a single, Petty's "Depot Street," was set to a reggae beat; it's a pleasant song, focused on dancing with one's sweetheart. The flipside, "Wild Eyes," was light rock, a bittersweet look at a failing relationship.

Tom later referred to the entire session as a "disaster," calling "Depot Street" a "novelty record." But on its release in 1975 (some sources say late 1974), it made *Billboard*'s "First Time Around" column, devoted to "new artists deserving of exposure." The magazine called the track a "Good reggae cut that fits in with current commercial standards." But beyond that positive nod, the single failed to chart.

Things began to fall apart for Mudcrutch. Danny Roberts, frustrated by Cordell's growing disinterest in the band, went back to Florida. Charlie Souza, bassist with Florida band the Tropics, was brought in to take over on bass. He arrived just in time for a recording session back in Tulsa, where one of the songs they worked on was a Petty number called "Don't Do Me Like That." Back in LA, Tom had a stint as a house sitter for Leon Russell. Mudcrutch was allowed to use his home studio, where "Hometown Blues" was first recorded.

But then the hammer fell. Tom was called in to meet with Cordell at Shelter's office. When he arrived, Denny told him Mudcrutch was being dropped, though he wanted Tom to stick around and pursue a career as a solo artist. Tom agreed, with one request; he wanted Mike Campbell retained as well (Campbell would eventually become Petty's indispensable right-hand man). Cordell said yes, and it was then left to Petty to tell the rest of the band they were dismissed. It was a discouraging end to Mudcrutch. "I had nothing, absolutely nothing to show for years of work," Tom later told his biographer. And then he tried to figure out what his next move should be.

"WE REALLY ARE AN LA BAND"

THE BIRTH OF THE HEARTBREAKERS

Tom catches that Pepsi spirit.

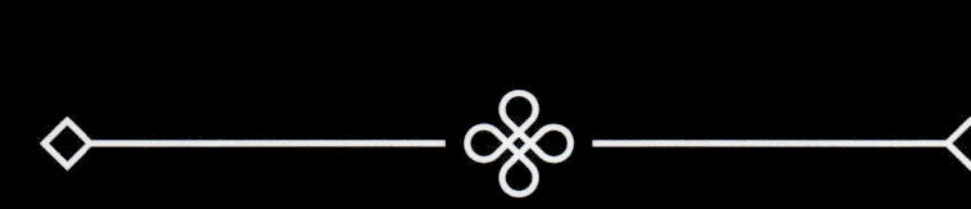

SPRING 1976

Tom was at loose ends. He'd come to LA with his wife Jane, who gave birth to their daughter, Adria, in November 1974. But now, with Tom having no band, Jane and Adria returned to Florida to live with her family until he could reestablish himself.

He still had his supporters. Denny Cordell signed him to a contract at a salary of $6,000 a year. Leon Russell, impressed by a Mudcrutch demo of "Lost in Your Eyes," reached out to Tom, suggesting they should write together, taking him around to various rock star homes and sessions. Russell also wanted to make an album with Petty. None of the planned projects ever materialized, but Tom considered the whole experience an invaluable education.

Tom also recorded songs with some of the area's top session players, but he found the results "too sterile." He didn't want to be a solo artist, working with pickup musicians, however good they were. He wanted to be in a band and explore the kind of creativity that could be generated by a group of people who worked together year after year.

In the meantime, the other members of Mudcrutch were keeping busy. Mike Campbell was working with Petty. Benmont Tench and Randall Marsh were playing in other bands. Tench was looking to get a new venture off the ground and was offered some studio time by a friend who worked at LA studio Village Recorders. He called up Tom asking if he'd come by the session to play harmonica. He also called Mike Campbell, Randall Marsh, and two other musicians from the Gainesville music scene who had made their way to Florida, guitarist Jeff Jourard and drummer Stan Lynch. Lynch invited another Gainesville musician to come along, bassist Ron Blair.

When Tom arrived at the session, it felt like old home week. He knew everybody in the room. He immediately felt comfortable working them; this was the kind of unified group he'd been hoping to find. He quickly set up another session with the musicians, working on the track "Strangered in the Night" (though Jim Gordon played drums on the track instead of Lynch or Marsh). Once Denny Cordell heard the new lineup, he agreed to take them on.

Ready for action: the first lineup of Tom Petty and the Heartbreakers, from left, Benmont Tench, Mike Campbell, Petty, Ron Blair, and Stan Lynch.

Tom had persuaded the other musicians to throw in their lot with him because he was signed to Shelter Records, so the newly formed band would already have a deal. But he hadn't planned on naming the group after himself. He'd suggested the King Bees as a possible name; the Gainesville All-Stars was another possibility. But with Tom as the one who had a deal with Shelter, Cordell wanted to keep the focus on him. So the band was given the name Tom Petty and the Heartbreakers.

There were a few lineup adjustments. There was no need for two drummers, and Cordell hadn't been that keen on Marsh's drumming during the Mudcrutch era, so he was out and Lynch was in. And three guitarists was at least one too many, so Jeff Jourard was out too, leaving a final lineup of Petty on lead vocals and rhythm guitar, Campbell on lead guitar, Blair on bass, Tench on keyboards, and Lynch on drums.

Cordell's business relationship with Leon Russell had fallen apart by this point, and Cordell was running Shelter on his own. To cut back on expenses, Cordell arranged for recording engineers to pick up some equipment from the studios in Tulsa and set up a studio next door to Shelter's LA offices. Petty and Lynch went along for the ride, and they ended up recording an early version of "Luna" in Tulsa. Then the gear was hauled to LA. "It seemed like the studio went up instantly," Tom later recalled. "And we were on our way."

07

"A SENSATIONAL NEW ARRIVAL"

TOM PETTY AND THE HEARTBREAKERS

NOVEMBER 9, 1976

Tom Petty in midflight at an early Heartbreakers show in Philadelphia.

One week the Heartbreakers were working in Shelter Records' rehearsal space. The next week the rehearsal space had become a recording studio, and the band was making their debut album.

While much of the album was recorded at Shelter's studio, some tracks that had been recorded earlier were also brought in. "Hometown Blues" had been recorded when Tom was housesitting for Leon Russell, and it featured Booker T. & the M.G.'s bassist Donald "Duck" Dunn on bass, Charlie Souza on sax, and Randall Marsh on drums. "Strangered in the Night" featured studio musicians Emory Gordy on bass and Jim Gordon on drums. Jeff Jourard also played guitar on a number of tracks before leaving the Heartbreakers.

But what became one of the most notable tracks came together during the Shelter sessions, with a little help from Dwight Twilley, of fellow Shelter act the Dwight Twilley Band. Mike Campbell had improvised what he called a "mindless doodle" of a riff during the fade-out of the song "Breakdown." When Twilley listened to a playback, he suggested making the riff more prominent throughout the track. Petty wisely took his advice, and Campbell's riff ended up being the key hook for this pensive number (the Dwight Twilley Band's Phil Seymour also provided backing vocals on the track; Seymour and Twilley sang on "Strangered in the Night" as well). It ended up becoming the Heartbreakers' first single.

The album's cover featured Tom, a smirk on his face, wearing a leather jacket with a belt of bullets draped around his neck. This gave some the erroneous impression that the Heartbreakers were a punk band (and it didn't help that there was an actual punk band with a similar name, Johnny Thunders and the Heartbreakers). But while the group shared the exuberant energy of punk, their music was born of classic rock influences. Petty said he wanted the band to have the harmonic melodicism of the Byrds and the swaggering rock of the Rolling Stones.

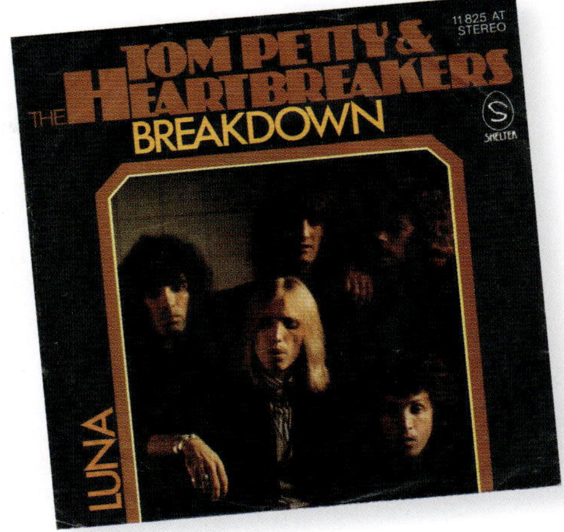

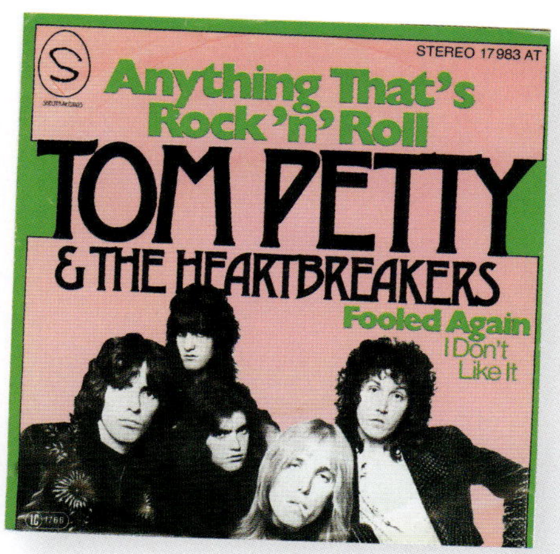

The album received mixed reviews. "Petty, another punk rock, black leather jacketed off shoot, delivers an assortment of sullen ballads and up tempo shriekers," wrote *Billboard,* though the reviewer did concede that on subsequent plays the vocals "become rather infectious." Sales-wise, the album got off to a slow start; in its first year, it only sold 12,000 copies. It would eventually attain gold status (sales of half a million)—but not until a decade after its release. Similarly, it wouldn't reach the *Billboard* chart for another two years, peaking at #55.

The story of how Jon Scott helped break the Heartbreakers on mainstream radio illustrates the persistence that it took to get the band wider recognition. In 1977, Scott had been hired as the head of album promotion at ABC Records (who distributed Shelter Records). He'd previously worked for MCA, where he'd got some radio play for Mudcrutch's "Depot Street." One day at his new job, he discovered a white label promo of the Heartbreakers' debut album in a closet, unaware it was by most of the musicians from Mudcrutch. He was thrilled on hearing "Breakdown," but was dismayed when his boss told him the album had come out eight months before, had done nothing, and that the band was probably getting dropped. "Don't drop this band without giving me a chance," Scott begged his boss. "Just give me six weeks." And then he got to work. Within a week, he had secured heavy rotation airplay on LA station KWST. The airplay led to a burst of new orders for the album from the chain store Tower Records. From there, support for "Breakdown" continued to grow, finally becoming the Heartbreakers' first US Top 40 single, peaking at #40 in 1978.

From the beginning, Petty's music sparked a fierce devotion among listeners, a loyalty that would eventually spread to fans around the world.

The Heartbreakers' first album got off to a slow start but eventually racked up sales over half a million. The band takes a break in San Francisco, 1979.

Tom at one of the first Heartbreakers shows in New York City.

BORN ON THE FOURTH OF JULY

Tom's debut album featured what would become his best-known song. The kind of song that people know even if they've never owned a single Tom Petty recording.

Petty wrote "American Girl" while living in Encino, near Leon Russell's house. The noise of the cars driving by on the freeway sounded like the ocean to him, or, as he put it in the song's second verse, the sound of "crashing on the beach." "The words just came tumbling out of me," he later told *Rolling Stone*. "The girl was looking for the strength to move on—and she found it."

It's a song of escape—of leaving the past behind to chase your dreams. And though the song's protagonist is female, it can also be read as autobiographical, telling Tom's own story. Especially as the setting seems to be his own home state of Florida; the lines referring to cars going by "on 441" is a reference to US Highway 441, a.k.a. the "Orange Blossom Trail," a 939-mile-long (1,55-km-long) highway that starts in Florida and passes through Gainesville on its way through Georgia, North Carolina, and Tennessee.

Some people even thought the lines were inspired by the suicide of a University of Florida student who jumped to her death from the Beaty Towers dormitory. Tom called the story an "urban legend," pointing out that the song's actual inspiration came from cars driving on a highway in California, not the South. Guitarist Mike Campbell also told *Songfacts*, "We used to have people come up to us and tell us they thought it was about suicide because of the one line about 'If she had to die,' but what they didn't get was, the whole line is, 'If she had to die *trying*.' Some people take it literally and out of context. To me it's just a really beautiful love song."

The song was recorded on July 4, 1976, at Shelter Records' studio. The jangling guitar and propulsive drumming launch the number with a brisk beat that never lets up, an element that made "American

"AMERICAN GIRL"

FEBRUARY 1977

"American Girl" quickly became one of the Heartbreakers signature songs.

The Heartbreakers at the Hammersmith Odeon (now the Eventim Apollo) onMay 15, 1977.

Girl" a live favorite. Though some assumed the chiming guitar sound was produced by a twelve-string guitar, it was actually Petty and Campbell playing six-string guitars simultaneously. In its final forty seconds, the tempo picks up in a glorious race to the finish line, with a fade-out that feels like it comes too soon; you'd rather keep on dancing.

"American Girl" brought the Heartbreakers' debut album to an upbeat close. It was also released as a single in early 1977, but failed to chart. It was reissued in 1994 to promote the *Greatest Hits* album, peaking at #109 in *Billboard*. By then the chart placing hardly mattered. It was considered one of Petty's best songs, and went on to be featured in numerous films and television shows, including *Fast Times at Ridgemont High*, *The Silence of the Lambs*, and *The Handmaid's Tale*.

The track's signature guitar sound makes more than one person think of the folk-rock group the Byrds—including the band's own Roger McGuinn, who, on first hearing "American Girl" joked, "When did I write that song?" He ended up covering it on his next album, *Thunderbyrd* (1977), making him one of the first artists to cover a Petty number. The song would subsequently be covered by such acts as Green Day, Def Leppard, the Shins, Goo Goo Dolls, and Taylor Swift, who turned in a very subdued acoustic version.

But none of them would surpass Tom's own version. Fittingly, it was the last song he performed with the Heartbreakers, at what turned out to be the band's final concert. As a *Billboard* headline put it, "'American Girl' Sums Up Everything Great About Tom Petty."

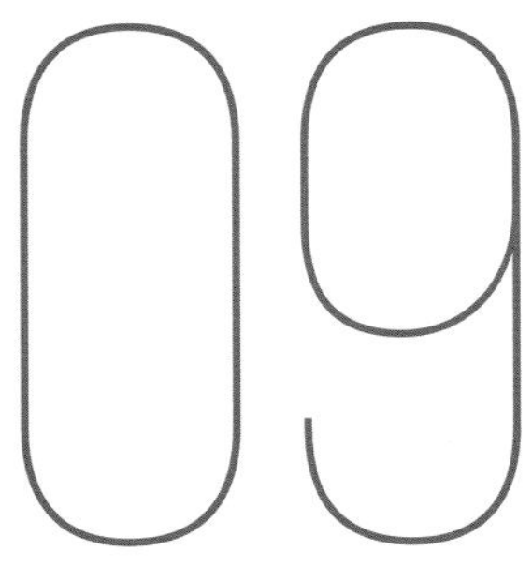

"ONE OF THE BEST NEW BANDS AROUND"

THE FIRST UK TOUR

MAY 8, 1977

Lead guitarist Mike Campbell, Tom's right-hand man in the band, plays a clear Lucite Ampeg Dan Armstrong guitar at London's Rainbow Theatre in June 1977.

Jimi Hendrix. Blondie. Tom Petty and the Heartbreakers. All are US musical performers who initially found greater commercial success in the UK than their native country.

The Heartbreakers' first US dates in 1976 and 1977 saw them opening for acts such as the Greg Kihn Band, Roger McGuinn, and one-off dates with Kiss and the Runaways. But they hadn't managed to really boost their profile outside of the greater LA area. Looking overseas, the band's British manager, Tony Dimitriades, showed a positive review of the Heartbreakers' debut album that had appeared in the UK music weekly *Sounds* to a London agent he knew. He wound up securing a UK tour for the Heartbreakers, opening for Nils Lofgren.

Sounds continued to hype the band and their leader. "You can quote me on this," Susin Shapiro wrote in April 1977: "Petty's going to be a big star, the new Heartbreak Kid of rock." But no one was prepared for how quickly things would take off. When the band arrived in the UK, the press was there to greet them, even though it was 7:30 in the morning. "And from there it was totally to the floor for two months," Petty told journalist Stephen Peeples. "I ran myself into the ground, completely."

The first show was at the Capitol Theatre in Cardiff, Wales. One attendee recalled it as a gig where the support act easily bested the headliner; the Heartbreakers "gave the crowd a set which Nils found difficult to follow. This was one of the rare occasions that I have seen the hall full for the first band, and the support act having to return for an encore." Petty was just as thrilled at the crowd response. "There were riots fifteen minutes into the first gig," he enthused to Peeples. "We'd never had people on stage knocking kids back down, and girls breaking through, knocking us around and grabbing us around the waist while we're trying to play. It's an incredible high."

Two days later, they were in London, on the TV music show *The Old Grey Whistle Test*—their first appearance on national television anywhere—performing "Listen to Her Heart." By the month's end, "Anything That's Rock 'n' Roll" was released as a UK-only single. UK music weekly *Melody Maker* proclaimed the Heartbreakers "one of the most in-demand bands playing in the country."

The United Kingdom gave the Heartbreakers their first taste of what their future success would feel like.

Tom holds his guitar aloft in triumph at a show at London's Rainbow Theatre, June 19, 1977.

After opening for Nils Lofgren, the Heartbreakers were given their own headlining tour.

The Heartbreakers then headed for Europe, where they appeared at the Pinkpop Festival in the Netherlands, delivered a forty-five-minute set on the German TV music show *Rockpalast*, and made stops in Belgium, France, and Sweden as well. Then it was back to the UK for more gigs.

Their sudden success had led to some awkward situations on the Lofgren tour; the Heartbreakers' unexpected popularity had generated enough bad feelings that Lofgren's roadies began leaving less and less space on stage for the Heartbreakers to set up their gear. But now the band was granted their own headlining tour, which took them through the end of June. They also appeared on the top TV music show in the country, *Top of the Pops*, lip-syncing to "Anything That's Rock 'n' Roll."

The touring paid off. *Tom Petty and the Heartbreakers* peaked at #24, "Anything That's Rock 'n' Roll" reached #36, and when "American Girl" was released later that summer, it peaked at #40, giving the Heartbreakers three Top 40 hits overseas before they'd had any such success in the United States. After the whirlwind trip, it was a comedown to return to the US, where the Heartbreakers hadn't taken off yet. As Tom later summarized for *Billboard*, "By the time we left England, we were a headlining band, and then we flew home and got off the plane, and you're nothing again." But it wouldn't take too long for that to change.

10

THE FIRST GOLD ALBUM

YOU'RE GONNA GET IT!

MAY 2, 1978

You're Gonna Get It! became the Heartbreakers' first gold album.

A long year and a half after releasing their debut album, the Heartbreakers finally returned with their second full-length release.

Not that they hadn't been busy in the meantime. They spent most of 1977 on the road, opening for other acts and occasionally headlining. They'd done their first overseas tour, taking in the UK and Europe. The band's last show of 1977 was a headlining spot at the Riviera Theater in Chicago on December 2. "Petty has learned much from a year of touring," *Rolling Stone* wrote in its review. "His tough-guy stares are now backed not only by stone-hard songs but also by his band's confidence."

The band devoted the first months of 1978 to focusing on making their second album; the next tour would be timed with the album's release. They hunkered down at Shelter Records' studio, and the hours were long. "I've spent so much time in the studio that the outside world has begun to look very strange to me," Tom later told *BAM* magazine's Blair Jackson. "I went out to a diner down the street the other night and I couldn't believe how disoriented I was."

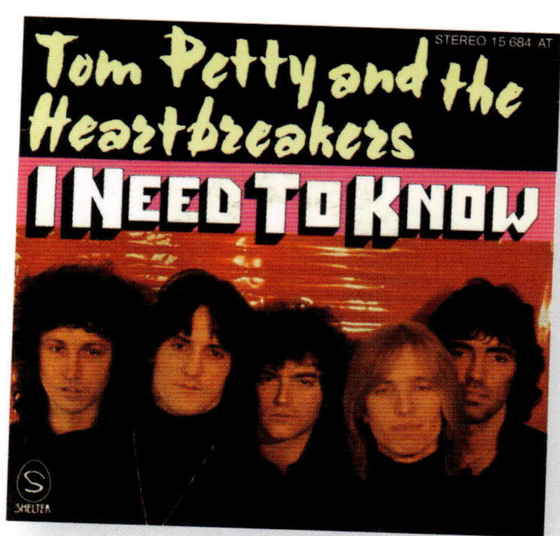

The hard work paid off. *You're Gonna Get It!* is a tight, well-paced album, clocking in at just under thirty minutes (indeed, a common complaint from fans would be that it was too short; they wanted to hear more). Both "Listen to Her Heart" and "I Need to Know" were already part of the band's setlist, both epitomizing the Heartbreakers' trademark sound of jangly guitars, catchy vocal harmonies, and solid pop hooks. "Hurt," one of two songs cowritten with Mike Campbell, further established the band as a West Coast act, as Tom sings about being glad he's heading home—to California.

Not that Petty was in any danger of forgetting his roots. The sweet "Magnolia" was, in his own description, "a Southern romantic song." It sets up a nice contrast with the title track, a tortured love song (with equally tortured vocal) with Tom cast as the spurned lover who is wishing ill fortune on his ex. And "Baby's a Rock 'n' Roller" (the album's other Petty/Campbell co-write) has some nice audio verité segments, with street sounds taped on cassette during a walk down Hollywood Boulevard dubbed onto the track to add a little atmosphere.

Terminal Romance was considered as the album's title, but it was ultimately replaced by the punchier *You're Gonna Get It!* It presented a more aggressive stance, something also reflected in the moody cover shot, with the band in blue, and the nervy intensity of tracks such as "When the Time Comes," which opens the album. "This is more of a *group record*," Petty emphasized to *BAM*. "The first record was us getting to know each other musically. I think this one has more depth, and I hope it's going to force more people to pick up on the fact that there really are five people involved with this group."

The album certainly met with a more positive reception than the Heartbreakers' debut, peaking at #23, though the singles still lagged behind ("I Need to Know" peaked at #41, "Listen to Her Heart" peaked at #59). The album also became Petty's first gold record—the first of what would eventually be a steady stream of awards and honors.

"Not only is *You're Gonna Get It!* more powerful and better-made than the group's first LP, it's one of the best rock albums I've heard in the last couple of years," Blair Jackson concluded in *BAM*. "If this album doesn't sell a million copies, there will be sufficient cause to worry about the health of this country." It wasn't quite the breakthrough the band wanted, but it was an album that definitely laid the groundwork for future success.

THE NATIONAL US TV DEBUT

THE MIDNIGHT SPECIAL

Though the Heartbreakers were touring more extensively, their first national US TV appearance gave them the opportunity to reach into every home across America.

The Midnight Special was a weekly music show on NBC that aired late at night, when most stations had signed off for the evening; there was no twenty-four-hour broadcasting in those days. A pilot episode aired on August 19, 1972, and, due to its success, the program was launched as a regular series on February 3, 1973, and ran through March 27, 1981. The ninety-minute episodes featured rotating hosts, contemporary music acts with a current hit single who performed live, and appearances by contemporary comics such as George Carlin and Richard Pryor.

As the program was geared toward a youthful demographic, it was the perfect platform for the Heartbreakers to promote their latest album, *You're Gonna Get It!* The program was taped on May 7, 1978, at NBC's studios in Burbank. As an Elvis fan, Tom may have relished the fact that it was the same venue where Presley had taped his landmark 1968 TV show *Singer Presents Elvis*, more commonly known as the "Comeback Special." The show's host for the episode was country star Crystal Gayle, who performed her biggest pop hit, "Don't It Make My Brown Eyes Blue." Chuck Mangione, Eddie

that Petty change the word "cocaine" to "champagne," as drug references wouldn't fly on the radio. Tom refused, saying that sparkling wine wasn't much of an inducement—"I mean, champagne is only $4 a bottle!" NBC had no such concerns, and Tom sang the line as written.

The up-tempo "I Need to Know" had the right kind of propulsive energy to let the band cut loose, a taut pop rocker that was a user-friendly two-and-a-half minutes (what *Cashbox* had noted as the song's hypnotic repeated hook worked especially well live). Rounding out things was "American Girl," already a concert staple, and the longest song of the short set.

Four days after taping their spot, the Heartbreakers launched their first extensive headlining tour, which took them up the West Coast, over to England for a few dates (including an appearance at the Knebworth Festival in Hertfordshire), then back to the US, where they'd continue to tour until the end of September. It would be over a year before they would make another national television appearance.

The *Midnight Special* gave Tom and the band a chance to get used to working in a new medium. In addition to raising the band's profile, it also gave their new release a boost. Whereas their debut album hadn't initially spun off any hit

The Midnight Special
BACKSTAGE PASS

Petty onstage in Los Angeles on June 4, 1978, two nights after the airing of the band's *Midnight Special* appearance.

12

"IT WAS A SURVIVAL TRIP"

BANKRUPTCY

MAY 23, 1979

All smiles in Santa Monica, California, even though a lawsuit is pending.

All Tom wanted to do was release his third album. Instead, he wound up in the middle of a lawsuit.

On March 4, 1979, ABC Records (who distributed Shelter Records) was acquired by MCA. Tom didn't like the idea of being "handed around to people we didn't know," and he contended that his contract gave him the right to have a say in who was going to distribute his records if the relationship between ABC Records and Shelter Records ever dissolved. Since it had now ended, he felt free from any further obligations to Shelter. So on March 12, Petty's management informed MCA that he would be looking for another label. "I've got nothing personally against MCA," Tom told Robert Hilburn of the *Los Angeles Times*, "except they tried to buy me without asking."

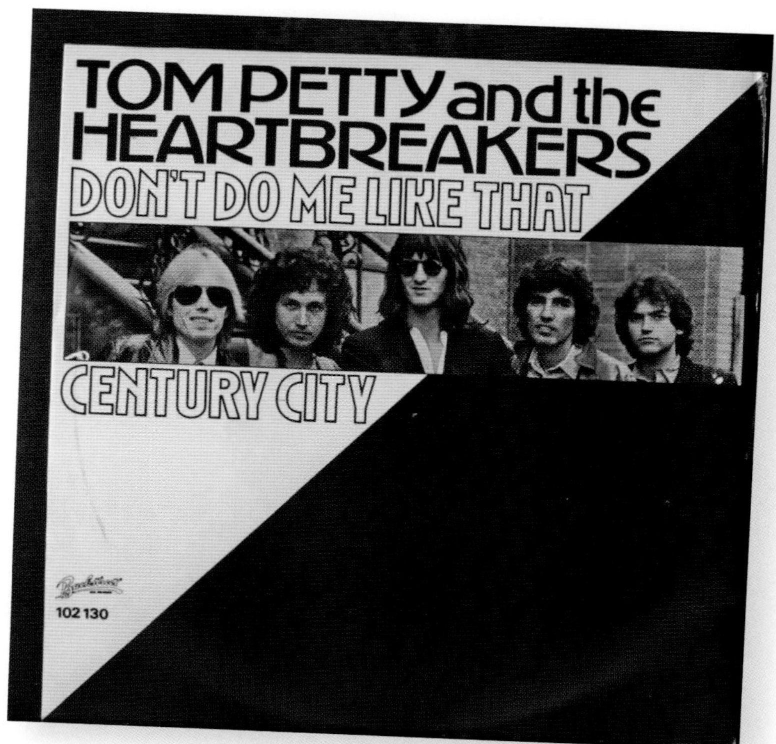

MCA's response was to file suit against him for breach of contract. The company also got a court order prohibiting Petty from negotiating with other labels.

Tom was having problems with Shelter Records as well. His first two albums had each been certified gold, and he'd notched up a handful of hit singles. Yet the money wasn't coming in from record sales or publishing. Tom hadn't fully appreciated the worth of publishing when he'd signed with Shelter. "So a fast one had been pulled on me, and I wanted to make it right," he explained. Tom was in the midst of making *Damn the Torpedoes*, but he had no plans to turn it in until the differences with MCA were settled. So Shelter Records sued him for breach of contract as well.

The battle lines were drawn. Work continued on the album, with the studio costs paid by Petty's comanager, Elliot Roberts. The tapes were removed from whatever studio the band was using after each session, so they wouldn't be seized by the record company. It was a fraught atmosphere for a creative endeavor, but the legal maneuverings did provide some inspiration for the song "Century City" (though Tom ultimately recast it as a love song, telling Hilburn, "I wouldn't want to write a song that was just about a lawsuit").

Then his legal advisors came up with a new strategy. In May, he filed a formal bankruptcy petition, claiming debts of $576,638 against $56,845 in assets. The rationale in filing for bankruptcy was that if Petty's current contracts wouldn't allow him to make the money to get out of debt, the court could readjust them. The danger was that, if Tom won, it could set a new precedent as a means by which artists could get out of their recording contracts. Naturally, record companies didn't want that to happen.

Though frustrated at having to spend so much of his time dealing with legal issues, Tom did manage to have a bit of fun with the situation. A short five-date tour of California was dubbed "The Lawsuit Tour," with T-shirts bearing that phrase among the merchandise for sale. But the bankruptcy ploy was also a gamble. Had Tom won in court, that victory might have kept other labels from wanting to work with him, fearful he might pull a similar stunt in the future.

But in the end, neither MCA or Shelter decided to risk the chance of handing recording artists the equivalent of a get out of jail free card, and they chose to settle. Tom agreed to sign with MCA, who, in a face-saving move, set up a special imprint, Backstreet Records, to release his recordings. Tom also got control of his publishing and a higher royalty rate. "We're in the best shape, financially, we've ever been in," he told *BAM* magazine.

"It was hard on everyone," Tom concluded about the lawsuit in the same interview, "but it's settled now and I think everyone is pretty happy about the way things turned out."

PART 2

INTO THE GREAT WIDE OPEN, 1979–1987

Petty and the Heartbreakers in Hollywood, circa 1987. From left, Howie Epstein, Stan Lynch, Petty, Benmont Tench, and Mike Campbell.

NUKES? NO!

THE MUSE BENEFIT PERFORMANCE

SEPTEMBER 22, 1979

A few months before the *Damn the Torpedoes* tour began, Tom made his first appearance at a major benefit concert, in support of MUSE—Musicians United for Safe Energy.

MUSE was founded by musicians Bonnie Raitt, Graham Nash, Jackson Browne, John Hall, and journalist/activist Harvey Wasserman. The organization was dedicated to raising awareness about the potential dangers of nuclear energy, particularly in the wake of the partial meltdown of the Three Mile Island Nuclear Generating Station near Harrisburg, Pennsylvania, on March 28, 1979, the worst accident in US commercial nuclear power plant history.

The organization's first large-scale event was a series of shows, The MUSE Concerts for a Non-Nuclear Future, which were held September 19 through 23 at Madison Square Garden. The multiday event aimed to tap into the progressive, counter-culture spirit of the 1960s, rallying people to a worthy cause. In addition to the four MUSE founders, the star-studded list of performers included Chaka Khan, Gil Scott-Heron, James Taylor, Carly Simon, Ry Cooder, and the biggest draw of the event, Bruce Springsteen.

On the night the Heartbreakers performed, the show began with sets by Raydio, Peter Tosh, and Bonnie Raitt and Rosemary Butler, who were joined by Jackson Browne on one song. Then came the Heartbreakers, placed in the hot seat—the set right before the Boss. It was also the first time the band had played Madison Square Garden. A further challenge was that the band had to make an impression with a shorter amount of time in which to do so.

But if the Heartbreakers felt any nerves, they readily rose to the challenge, turning in a tight, energetic, nine-song set. "I Need to Know" gets the proceedings off to an upbeat start, a mood and tempo maintained with the next selection, "Anything That's Rock 'n' Roll." Then came a preview of *Damn the Torpedoes*, the album that was less than a month away from release. "This is a new song," was Tom's simple introduction to what would be one of the album's most acclaimed tracks, "Refugee," burning with intensity and confidence. It was followed by

After his own set at the MUSE antinuke event, Tom joined Bruce Springsteen during the Boss's set, doing a cover "Stay" alongside Jackson Browne.

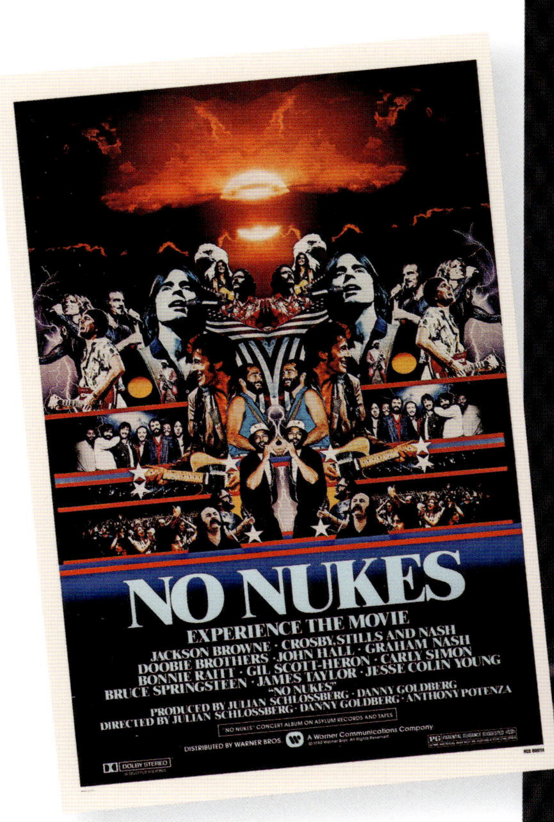

"American Girl," already a mainstay of the Heartbreakers' live shows, and always a crowd pleaser.

And then came a surprise, a crossover into sweet soul music with a cover of Solomon Burke's "Cry to Me." It was a great way to demonstrate the Heartbreakers' musical versatility (this was no group of one-note rock 'n' rollers), not to mention Tom's impassioned vocal performance. Then it was back to the gritty side of the street with "Strangered in the Night," followed by the unmistakable opening drumbeat of "Breakdown," with the band turning in a haunting, brooding rendition, with ad-libbed lyrics and a careful fade-out at the end.

The tempo then rockets forward again for the final two songs, "Too Much Ain't Enough," and a rollicking version of the Isley Brothers' "Shout," a terrific rocker that Petty often dropped into his shows. Toni Lenz, in *The Montclarion*, praised the band's set, calling it "rocking, tight, and just the right amount of time"; clearly, no fans of the Boss were going to say that Tom had overstayed his welcome. Nor was he done for the night, for he, Jackson Browne, and Rosemary Butler returned during Springsteen's set to join him in a terrific cover of "Stay," a doowop classic by Maurice Williams and the Zodiacs.

The MUSE concert saw Tom as part of a star-studded bill that not only included Springsteen and Browne, but also Bonnie Raitt, James Taylor, Carly Simon, and Crosby, Stills & Nash.

The live album *No Nukes: The MUSE Concerts for a Non-Nuclear Future* was released in November 1979 and featured the Heartbreakers' "Cry to Me"; it reached #14 in the US. It was the first official release of live material by the band; the 1977 EP, *Official Live 'Leg*, was a promotional release, not sold to the general public. A concert film, *No Nukes*, was released but featured no footage of the Heartbreakers. The complete Heartbreakers' performance has never been released officially, but it can be found on the internet.

14

"THE ALBUM WE'VE ALL BEEN WAITING FOR"

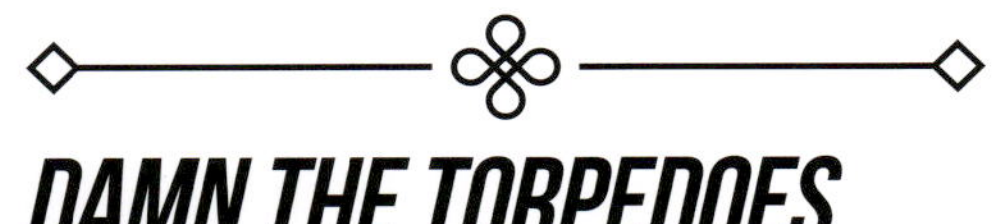

DAMN THE TORPEDOES

OCTOBER 19, 1979

It was the breakthrough record that was a long time coming—which made its arrival all the sweeter. *Damn the Torpedoes* would be Tom's first album to hit the Top 10. The first album to be certified platinum, for sales of over 1 million (it would eventually sell over 3 million copies in the US). And the critical plaudits didn't hurt either.

When Tom and the Heartbreakers began work on their third album, they were determined to take their music to the next level. This album would be quite different from the two that proceeded it, starting with the studio environment, for it would mark the first time the group had worked in a 24-track studio. "One big difference was that we used a big room to record in; we've always used little rooms in the past," Tom explained to *Record Review*. "We used a big room to cut the tracks, to get live echo, real echo, and we could play louder, more like we do live. All we did was play almost two dozen songs until we had the feel and the arrangements the way we wanted."

It wasn't quite that simple. The sessions proved to be fraught, and not just because of the legal difficulties surrounding the band. Danny Cordell had produced the first Heartbreakers album; he shared that credit with Noah Shark and Tom on the second. Now there was a new man in the producer's chair: Jimmy Iovine.

(Left)
Jimmy Iovine with Stevie Nicks. Petty and Iovine bonded straightaway, though Iovine put drummer Stan Lynch "through the fucking ringer," according to Benmont Tench.

The future cofounder of Interscope Records and Beats Electronics got his start working as an engineer on John Lennon's *Walls and Bridges* and Bruce Springsteen's *Born to Run* albums. He had also produced Patti Smith's *Easter* album, and Tom loved the sound on "Because the Night" in particular. Iovine was originally hired as an engineer, but he took over the producer's role by simply bringing in his own engineer, Shelly Yakus.

Petty and Iovine quickly bonded. "We must have talked on the phone every night for a year," Tom later recalled to author Warren Zanes. There was plenty to discuss. What songs should be on the album? How should it sound? What could they do in the studio that hadn't been tried before? Jimmy had an opinion about everything. He and Yakus even put up the money to get Tom a better home stereo system.

But Iovine also pushed the band harder than they'd ever been worked before in the studio, demanding take after take. He was particularly unhappy with Stan Lynch's drumming, which ultimately led to Lynch being fired. He was soon rehired, but the bad feelings lingered. Benmont Tench felt the later difficulties the band had with Lynch started with these sessions: "Jimmy and Shelly put Stan through the fucking ringer."

The pending lawsuit also hung over the sessions like a sword of Damocles waiting to drop; would they even get to release this album? Tom admitted the legal proceedings had an influence, telling *BAM*, "You could probably find a lot of things that could be interpreted as references to the legal thing. . . . But I hope that people don't sit down with the record and look for it. I've tried not to limit the songs to those kinds of interpretations." And, as he jokingly pointed out, "Most of my songs are just about girls."

Whatever the song's themes, *Damn the Torpedoes* proved to be an album of classic rock staples, with Iovine's clean, crisp production making the band sound better than they ever had before. The album reached #2, kept out of the top spot by Pink Floyd's blockbuster *The Wall* ("It made me hate Pink Floyd," Tom joked). As *Orange Coast Magazine* observed, "With this release, the record-buying public is finally discovering what the critics have known for years, that T.P. and the boys are rock 'n' roll at its finest."

Co-written with Campbell, "Here Comes My Girl" was the third single from *Torpedoes*. It reached No. 59 in the US.

Petty and the Heartbreakers onstage at the Tower Theatre in Philadelphia, Pennsylvania, a month after the release of *Damn the Torpedoes*, November 13, 1979. The show would provide the hook for Mikal Gilmore's *Rolling Stone* feature the following spring.

15

“A SOLID POP SINGLES GROUP”

THE FIRST TOP 20 HITS

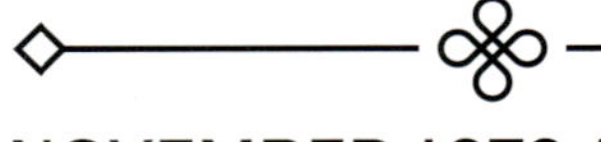

NOVEMBER 1979 AND JANUARY 1980

Tom playing the Poplar Creek Music Theater in Hoffman Estates, Illinois, on June 18, 1980.

In addition to its success on the album chart, *Damn the Torpedoes* gave Tom his first big successes on the US singles chart as well.

"Don't Do Me Like That" was chosen as the first single, to Tom's surprise (he would've preferred "Here Comes My Girl"). The song had been written and recorded during the Mudcrutch era; that early version was later released on the *Playback* box set in 1995. It's a straight-forward plea to a loved one, saying: don't do me wrong. Tom explained that the title phrase was something his father used to say.

Guitarist Mike Campbell said it took a long time to perfect "Refugee," to the point where he briefly walked out of the session.

It was also the hit that almost got away. After Mudcrutch broke up, the recording went into the vault and Tom had no thoughts of revisiting it. When Jimmy Iovine found the song while searching through Tom's archives during the recording of *Damn the Torpedoes*, Tom told him he thought it was better suited to a group like the J. Geils Band. Certainly the song's taut, punchy rhythms would have made it a good fit for the group best known for the hit "Centerfold." But Iovine was quick to persuade Petty to keep it for himself; how could he possibly give away a song with such potential?

So the Heartbreakers ended up recording a new version of the song. In contrast to the original, it exudes far more confidence and musical proficiency. And unlike "Breakdown," which had taken a year to get into the US charts, "Don't Do Me Like That" was an immediate hit on its release, quickly landing at #10. "I think it's the best song we've ever done," Tom said at the time of its release.

Some Petty fans might disagree, giving that honor to another *Torpedoes* song, "Refugee," considered one of his most notable numbers. The music had been written by Mike Campbell; Tom completed the song by listening to Campbell's cassette demo, as he paced around the room, the lyrics coming quickly, in about twenty minutes. And though ostensibly about a romantic relationship, Tom conceded the lyrics also reflected his "defiant mood" of the time, when he was caught up in the lawsuit with MCA and Shelter Records, as can be heard in the pointed references to the need to "fight to be free."

But though written quickly, "Refugee" took considerable time to record. "We just had a hard time getting the feel right," Mike Campbell told *Songfacts*. "We must have recorded that one hundred times." Tom said it was producer Iovine who demanded such perfection: "He wouldn't accept less than greatness." Eventually, Campbell grew so frustrated he walked out of the session. It turned out to be a necessary break; when he returned, the track was completed quickly.

By then, everyone had come to recognize just how powerful a track "Refugee" was. "You know that certain things are better than others that you've done and you notice that the band or the people around start responding to it more than certain songs," explained Campbell. "You can tell that maybe there's something special about this one." Final confirmation of that came while they were mixing the song, catching the attention of one of the studio's receptionists who said, "That's a hit." "And we looked at each and said, 'Maybe it is,'" Campbell recalled.

On its release, *Billboard* praised the "passionate rocker highlighted by Petty's gutsy rock vocal and searing guitar lines," and the song reached #15. It was followed by "Here Comes My Girl," which, though receiving good reviews, stalled at #59. No matter. Petty and the Heartbreakers had firmly established themselves as a force to be reckoned with.

"LIVE, FROM NEW YORK, IT'S . . ."

FIRST *SATURDAY NIGHT LIVE* APPEARANCE

NOVEMBER 10, 1979

In the 1950s and 1960s, appearing on *The Ed Sullivan Show* was a sign that you had really made it in the entertainment business. In the 1970s, at least for rock acts, that honor passed to *Saturday Night Live*.

Saturday Night Live (*SNL*) made its debut on NBC on October 11, 1975 (it was then called *NBC's Saturday Night*). The late night show featured comedy sketches and parody commercials, done by a young, hip cast; the original regulars included future stars Gilda Radner, Chevy Chase, Jane Curtain, and John Belushi. Shows also featured a musical guest. George Carlin was the host for *SNL*'s first episode, with musical guests Janis Ian and Billy Preston.

Tom made his first *SNL* appearance the month after *Damn the Torpedoes*' release; Buck Henry was the show's host. The band was casually dressed, in suit jackets and open-necked shirts. Tom added a splash of color by wearing a red shirt. "Don't Do Me Like That," just released as a single, was an obvious selection. The band also performed "Refugee." They're both strong, confident performances, the band clearly more comfortable before television cameras than they'd previously been.

Petty went on to appear on *SNL* seven more times, making him one of the program's more frequent musical guests. For his February 19, 1983, appearance, he performed "The Waiting" and "Change of Heart." On May 20, 1989, he chose to perform "Runnin' Down a Dream" and "Free Fallin'," much to his record label's frustration; MCA had hoped he'd perform his current hit single, "I Won't Back Down." "But my thinking was, 'I Won't Back Down' was already a hit, let's play something they don't expect," he later told *Billboard*. "I'm sure it helped the record later. Sometimes you just gotta do what you think is right." As it turned out, the songs he performed on the show were both later released as singles.

On his October 12, 1991, appearance, he performed "Into the Great Wide Open" and "King's Highway." His November 19, 1994, appearance attracted a lot of attention, as it marked Nirvana drummer Dave Grohl's first major live appearance since the death of the band's lead singer/guitarist Kurt Cobain the previous April. Petty's appearance had been booked before Stan Lynch left the band, so a replacement drummer needed to be found quickly. When Grohl was offered the slot, he was surprised: "My first reaction was, 'What the fuck? He couldn't find a real drummer?'" Petty even asked Grohl to replace Lynch full time, but Grohl had just completed the first Foo Fighters album and decided he'd rather strike out on his own. But you can see what might've been in the performances of "You Don't Know How It Feels" and "Honey Bee."

The September 28, 1996, appearance featured "Walls" and "Angel Dream." The April 10, 1999, appearance featured "Swingin' and "Room at the Top." His last appearance, on May 15, 2010, featured "I Should Have Known It" and "Jefferson Jericho Blues." Tom also put in a blink-and-you'll-miss-it cameo in a comedic song performed during the show by Andy Samberg.

And there was an unexpected tribute to Petty in the opening sequence of *SNL*'s October 7, 2017, episode. It was six days after a mass shooting at the Route 91 Harvest music festival in Las Vegas, which occurred while country music star Jason Aldean was performing. Now Aldean stood center stage on the *SNL* set, remarking "Like everyone, I'm struggling to understand what happened that night and how to pick up the pieces and start to heal." Then he performed a number that had a new poignancy, given that Tom had died just three days earlier. It was Petty's own song of inner strength, "I Won't Back Down."

Petty and his Vox teardrop guitar take the stage at New York City's Palladium on November 11, 1979, the night after their first *SNL* appearance.

17

"I FELT LIKE I HAD ARRIVED"

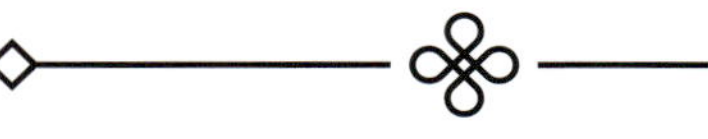

THE FIRST *ROLLING STONE* COVER

FEBRUARY 21, 1980

Tom blew out his voice at this show in Philadelphia in November 1979, a cramatic occurrence that provided the opening for Mikal Gilmore's 1980 *Rolling Stone* cover story.

In early 1980, Tom was in a hospital in Santa Monica, recovering from a bout of tonsillitis. Then a visitor came by with an unexpected gift: the latest issue of *Rolling Stone*—with himself on the cover.

It was the first time he'd graced the cover of the magazine, and he admitted it was a thrill, exactly how the experience is referred to in the song "The Cover of 'Rolling Stone'" by Dr. Hook & the Medicine Show (released as a single in October 1972, the song reached #6 in early 1973, and the band got their wish when an illustration of the group appeared on the cover of *Rolling Stone*'s March 29, 1973 issue). And it boded well for Petty's future. The Heartbreakers' first two albums had been well-received, but they were not big sellers. Now, *Damn the Torpedoes* had kicked the doors open, and getting the cover of *Rolling Stone* confirmed that Tom, and the Heartbreakers, were stars.

The story, "Tom Petty's Real-Life Nightmares," was written by Mikal Gilmore and featured photos by Annie Leibovitz. As revealed in the subtitle, "A Travelogue Of Lost Hope, Broken Dreams, Disillusion And, Finally, Renewal," captured Petty and his band on the road, touring in support of their latest album. In dramatic fashion, the story opens with Tom blowing his voice out during his November 13, 1979, show at the Tower Theater in Philadelphia, three nights after making his *Saturday Night Live* appearance. "I was afraid something like this could happen," Petty's comanager Tony Dimitriades is quoted as saying. But after a ten-minute break, the band was back onstage and managed to complete their set "with an all-or-bust determination." "I fucked up a gig because I was out doing interviews," Tom groused the next day, a remark that made Gilmore feel "like a medical liability." That evening's concert was rescheduled to a later date to allow Petty's throat to recover.

Gilmour eventually got his interview when Petty was in better spirits. The article captures Tom during a transitional period, as he moved from regional success to national fame. Once his voice was in working order, Petty proves to be intelligent and thoughtful about life in the music industry. He sounds relieved to have left the miseries of the lawsuits behind him, though acknowledging the frustration provided some inspirational fuel for *Damn the Torpedoes*. He's also quick to point out the new pressures he's having to deal with, stating how he'd like to cut back on interviews ("I have days now when I simply *can't* sit down and dredge up all those same responses over and over").

He astutely points out the self-defeating trap of feeling that each record has to top the one before ("If you let that mentality overtake you, you end up being one of those people who is afraid to run off course"). And he's self-deprecating about his own work ("I mean, it's only rock & roll—just disposable crap that won't mean much in ten years"). Gilmore begs to differ; he's a big fan of *Damn the Torpedoes*, calling it "easily Petty and the Heartbreakers' most cohesive and resplendent effort," comparing it to Bruce Springsteen's *Darkness on the Edge of Town*, about "people cut off from their wishes but not their pride."

Tom would grace the cover of *Rolling Stone* another six times (including once with Bob Dylan, and on the magazine's 1,000th issue, which featured a star-studded crowd of rock personalities). But there's nothing like your first time. And to the larger rock audience it confirmed that Tom Petty was no longer simply "promising"; he was a bona fide star.

It's likely every musician has dreamed of being on the cover of *Rolling Stone*. It became a reality for Tom in 1980.

Back on the boards in London at the Hammersmith Odeon on March 6, 1980.

TOP OF THE CHARTS

“THE WAITING”

APRIL 20, 1981

Though it only reached #19 on *Billboard*'s Hot 100, "The Waiting" still managed to give Tom his first chart topper on the magazine's Mainstream Rock Tracks chart.

The song is unabashedly romantic—a mid-tempo number about the pain of the long, long wait before "the one" comes into your life, and the relief when they finally do. Tom explained that the inspiration for the chorus came from a quote he thought he'd heard by Janis Joplin: "I love being onstage, and everything else is just waiting." Roger McGuinn insisted he'd made a similar comment to Tom. But the notion that there are moments when you truly feel alive is a common one. Joplin's comment sounds like a variation of the quote first attributed to high-wire performer Karl Wallenda, who was said to have made the observation, "Life is on the wire; everything else is just waiting."

Unusually, it was the chorus that had come first to Tom, which was not how he usually composed a number, preferring instead to start at the beginning and work his way through to the end. "It's a whole lot harder to work back from the chorus," he told author Paul Zollo, and it took a number of weeks for him to finish the song. Another unusual aspect is that Petty celebrates his new love in the verses, but makes the anticipation of waiting the focus of the chorus. A more conventional approach would be to have the waiting described in the verses with the emotional payoff of finally connecting with your loved one coming in the chorus. But ultimately, Petty's approach is the stronger one; there's a bittersweet resonance to his singing about waiting being the "hardest part" that tugs at your heartstrings.

The song's video is a straightforward performance by the band, who play while standing on a series of white steps artfully splattered with paint. In a nice bit of *cinema verité*, at the song's end, the band stops miming while the music continues to play, keyboardist Benmont Tench and drummer Stan Lynch swap instruments, and the film crew wanders onto the set.

"The Waiting" quickly became a live favorite, in part because the song's "yeah yeah" call-and-response setup before the chorus kicks in was tailormade for audience participation. In fact, it was this section in particular that brought home to Replacements' lead singer/guitarist Paul Westerberg, during a tour where his band opened for the Heartbreakers, why Petty's band was so commercially successful—and why Westerberg's was not. The sound of thousands of fans eagerly singing "Yeah, yeah!" as the Heartbreakers performed "The Waiting" made him reflect, "maybe we just weren't made of the stuff that makes popular music."

Producer Jimmy Iovine, for one, considered "The Waiting" a stronger song

Tom was successful at keeping the record company from adding a dollar to the retail price of *Hard Promises*, an accomplishment he celebrated in this puckish photo.

than "Refugee," "so when it wasn't a hit, a real hit, it killed me. It was devastating. I felt it was as good as anything I'd been near." There was a suspicion that the release of "Stop Draggin' My Heart Around" (Stevie Nicks' single that also featured Petty and the Heartbreakers) as a single had killed the momentum for singles from the Heartbreakers' own record, radio programmers perhaps feeling that the band was already getting enough exposure.

But if it was a disappointment that "The Waiting" wasn't a bigger hit, it had still copped the top spot on at least one chart, meaning the Heartbreakers could legitimately claim they were now a number one band. It was the first of six times Tom would hit #1 on the Mainstream Rock Tracks chart. And he would steadily make inroads on the Hot 100 as well.

TOM PETTY AND THE HEARTBREAKERS
THE WAITING
HARD PROMISES

19

"PETTY'S WRITING HAS GROWN ENORMOUSLY"

HARD PROMISES

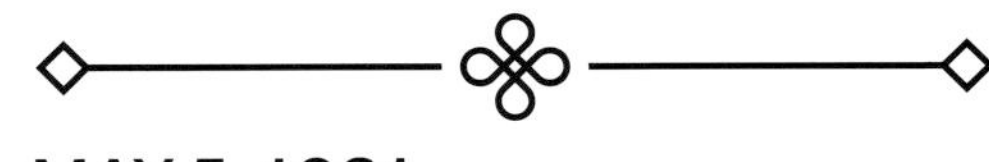

MAY 5, 1981

Ready to roll: the Heartbreakers pause in Chicago during their 1981 tour of the US.

When you've finally had a highly successful record, there can be a lot of pressure when it comes time to make the follow-up. But for Tom, simply the fact that there was no ongoing lawsuit to deal with while recording meant that the making of *Hard Promises* was definitely less stressful.

But he did put a lot of thought into how he wanted this album to improve on the band's previous work. "I just wanted to up the quality," he told Dave Marsh. "I've always felt that we looked a little dumber than we are, to the public. With this record, I felt, we've gone through so much and seen so much, and there's so much to this, we can't play dumb and make another record of teenage love songs."

Certainly there weren't any tracks that would fall into that category. *Hard Promises* was an album that evinced a new maturity. "Insider," originally written for Stevie Nicks, is a moving ballad about the end of a relationship (a line in the chorus provided the album's title). Nicks shares the vocal with Petty, and she also contributed vocals to the album's closing track, "You Can Still Change Your Mind."

The mid-tempo rocker "A Woman in Love (It's Not Me)" has a nuanced storyline, with the narrator an observer of a relationship headed for destruction. The taut, funky "Nightwatchman" reflected the realities of newfound fame in Tom's life; he now needed a security guard to keep people off his front lawn. The *New York Times'* Robert Palmer, noting that the album had a more pessimistic outlook than its predecessor, praised Petty's "fine, terse" songwriting style, comparing it to the works of hardboiled mystery writer Raymond Chandler.

At one point during the recording, there was excitement about the fact that John Lennon was expected to arrive at the same studio the Heartbreakers were using, to work on songs for fellow Beatle Ringo Starr's album. So everyone was devastated when Lennon was murdered on December 8, 1980. In tribute, the words "We Love You J.L." were etched in the runout groove of first pressings of *Hard Promises*.

And there was another kerfuffle with MCA when the label decided to apply

Tom poses with his Gibson Everly Brothers model acoustic guitar for famed rock photographer Lynn Goldsmith in 1981, around the release of *Hard Promises*, his second Top 10 album.

what they called "superstar pricing" to the Heartbreakers' new album; instead of $8.98, the price tag would be $9.98. This was not at all to Tom's liking. "My immediate reaction was 'No way,'" he told *Rolling Stone*. "It just ain't right. I don't need the extra dollar, and I can't imagine that MCA needs it." Not that it was a fight he'd wanted to pick. "For once in my life, I'd like to make a record without a legal battle," he told *Ampersand*, which also quoted the snippy response from an MCA representative: "Maybe if he didn't burn up a million dollars making the record it wouldn't have to cost so much."

But he also had some fun, threatening to title the album *Eight Ninety Eight* in retaliation. And by the time he was pictured on the cover of *Rolling Stone*'s July 23, 1981, issue, wearing a suit and tie and smiling as he rips a dollar bill in half, MCA had capitulated; *Hard Promises* would have a list price of $8.98. Tom also had a further last laugh. The album's cover shows him in a record store, standing by a crate of albums selling for—$8.98. "It was just too irresistible to not do a little—retouching," he joked.

Commercially, the album did less well than *Damn the Torpedoes*, peaking at #5, and selling over a million copies. The singles "The Waiting" and "A Woman in Love (It's Not Me)" reached #19 and #79, respectively.

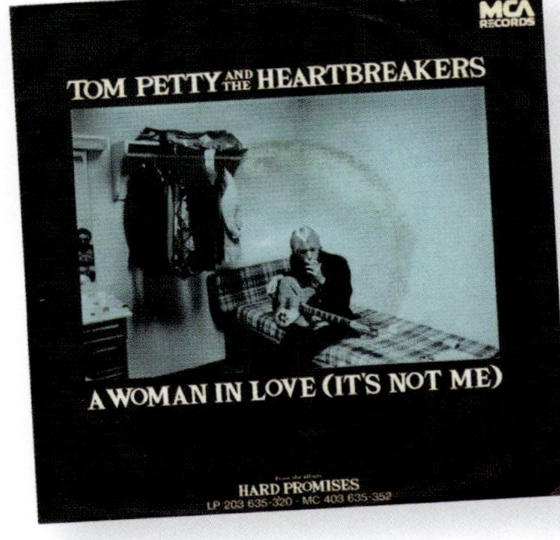

Hard Promises would also be the last album released by the original Petty-Campbell-Tench-Blair-Lynch Heartbreakers lineup. Changes were on the horizon.

20

"ROCK AND ROLL HEAVEN"

Stevie Nicks, who said she'd have loved to join the Heartbreakers, did the next best thing by making regular guest appearances with the band.

"STOP DRAGGIN' MY HEART AROUND"

JULY 8, 1981

It all began with "Insider."

Fleetwood Mac's Stevie Nicks was a huge fan of Tom Petty and the Heartbreakers. As she later told *Rolling Stone*, after hearing the band's debut album, "I became such a fan that if I hadn't been in a band myself, I would have joined that one."

Stevie obviously wasn't going to be able to join the Heartbreakers. So when she began work on her debut solo album, 1981's *Bella Donna*, she did the next best thing: she asked Tom to produce it. Tom initially agreed and worked with her on the track "Outside the Rain." But he ultimately decided he didn't want the job; he'd been put off by her entourage that hung around during the sessions. So, he recommended his own producer, Jimmy Iovine, instead. Iovine not only ended up producing the album, he and Nicks also became a couple.

But Tom did agree to write a song for Stevie and came up with "Insider." Iovine was especially enthusiastic about it, saying, "That's the best fucking song you ever wrote!" While recording her part, Stevie began harmonizing with Tom's guide vocal as she listened to it over the headphones. Tom gave contradictory accounts of what happened next. He told writer Dave Marsh that Stevie could tell from his reaction that he wanted to keep the song for himself, and she offered to give it back to him. "I really thought a lot of her for that," Petty said. But in

Conversations with Tom Petty, he says that he asked for the track back himself.

In either case, he also agreed to give her another song he'd recorded with the Heartbreakers, "Stop Draggin' My Heart Around," cowritten with Mike Campbell. On hearing it, Stevie was quickly won over, telling Tom, "Wow! That's why I wanted you to write me a song—it's rock 'n' roll, that's what *you* do. 'Insider' sounds like what I do." It would be the album's only song that Nicks didn't write or co-write.

The Heartbreakers could be found all over *Bella Donna*. Benmont Tench played organ on eight of the album's nine tracks; Petty, Campbell, and Stan Lynch all turned up on "Outside the Rain," and Campbell put in another appearance on "The Highwayman." But it was "Stop Draggin' My Heart Around," the album's first single, that made the biggest impact. The song reached #3, the highest chart placing the Heartbreakers ever received in *Billboard*'s Hot 100. The song's video, featuring the performers miming in a studio setting, was the twenty-fifth video played on MTV's inaugural day, August 1, 1981.

The video also underscores why the song works better as a duet than it would have as a solo number. Instead of it being one person disappointed in their romantic partner, the song depicts two people grappling with a turbulent relationship, thus heightening the drama. In perhaps the best sign of its influence, satirist "Weird Al" Yankovic did a parody version of the song called "Stop Draggin' My Car Around," though there was, alas, no accompanying video.

Tom and Stevie ended up becoming good friends. He teamed up with her again on "I Will Run to You" from her second solo album, *The Wild Heart*, in 1983. And in 2006, Stevie finally fulfilled her dream of becoming a Heartbreaker. She made several appearances on the band's thirtieth anniversary tour that year, and Tom presented her with a special item in commemoration: a platinum sheriff's badge, studded with diamonds, that read "To Our Honorary Heartbreaker, Stevie Nicks" on the front, and "To the Only Girl in Our Band" on the back. "It goes with me everywhere," she said. "It's probably the most beautiful piece of jewelry a man has ever given me, ever."

Tom Petty and Stevie Nicks started out as musical colleagues and became lifelong friends.

"IT CHANGED EVERYTHING"

"YOU GOT LUCKY" VIDEO

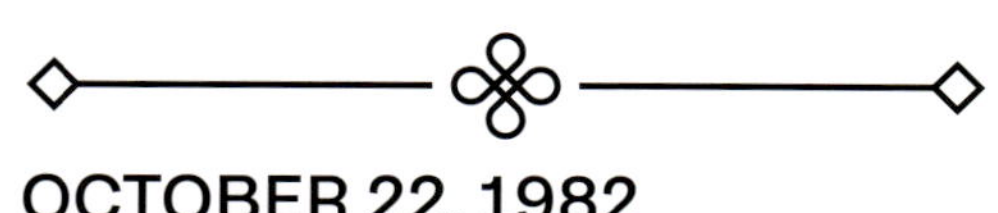

OCTOBER 22, 1982

Tom had been making videos for his singles since the release of "Refugee." But they had simply captured the band in a straightforward performance. For "You Got Lucky," Tom and the Heartbreakers decided to up their game.

Musicians had been making short clips of themselves in performance for decades. In the 1930s, as sound films replaced silent movies, live-action shorts of musical acts were made to show before the main feature. In the 1940s, "Soundies" were musical shorts that could be viewed on coin-operated machines, a concept updated for the 1960s with Scopitone machines. The 1960s also saw the rise of what were called promotional films, short film clips of a music act in performance that were sent around for broadcast on TV variety shows. The Beatles were among the artists who began to experiment with the format, releasing promo films in which they weren't seen lip-syncing—a novel idea at the time.

Then, on August 1, 1981, the cable network MTV (Music Television) was launched, the world's first station broadcasting music promo films twenty-four hours a day, making the demand for such films jump dramatically. The clips also became known as "music videos" as they were now more frequently shot on video and thus less expensive than shooting on film (eventually all clips, whether shot on video or film, were generically referred to as music videos).

"You Got Lucky" was directed by Jim Lenahan, a former member of Mudcrutch who went on to be the Heartbreakers' lighting director. He had directed several of the band's previous videos. The action is set in a postapocalyptic desert wasteland, a look that was heavily influenced by the *Mad Max* films (the actual location was Vasquez Rocks Natural Area Park, in northern Los Angeles County). In an unusual setup, the video has an introductory prologue that runs for over a minute before the music begins, as Petty and Mike Campbell pull up in a hovercar (from the TV series *Logan's Run*) and come across a boombox wrapped in plastic. Michael Jackson was so impressed with the notion of a video featuring an introduction that he called Petty up to enthuse about what an "incredible idea" it was, later giving his video for "Thriller" its own memorable introduction.

The tape player is turned on, the music starts, and the rest of the band arrives via a futuristic motorcycle complete with sidecar. But though the band wanders into a mysterious tent that's full of musical and recording equipment, and Campbell picks up a guitar to play the song's guitar solo, there's no other miming; the band is more interested in examining the adjacent video games. The only time the Heartbreakers are seen performing is in the random footage (drawn from their previous videos) that plays on a bank of TV monitors also in the tent, mixed in with clips from the TV series *Galactica 1980*. At the end, the band members return to their vehicles and drive away, Petty leaving the boombox by the side of the road.

"You Got Lucky" reached #20 in *Billboard*'s main chart, and #1 in the magazine's Mainstream Rock Tracks chart. And the video proved to be a turning point in how the band would utilize the format in the future. Musicians generally regarded making videos as an unwelcome promotional chore, but Tom quickly realized that you could be as creative in a video as you were in making music. It also greatly expanded your potential audience. "That was when we really saw MTV change our daily lives," Tom said about the "You Got Lucky" video. "Not only were teenagers spotting me on the street, older people would spot me, too. We knew it was big."

The band plays Germany in late 1982. Mike Campbell's hat (background) and Tom's bandana appear to take inspiration from the "You Got Lucky" video.

22

"PETTY'S MOST ACCOMPLISHED RECORD"

LONG AFTER DARK

NOVEMBER 2, 1982

Tom, photographed with one of his beloved Rickenbacker guitars in 1982,called *Long After Dark* the album where he got back to "doing rock 'n'roll stuff."

Tom had some ambivalence about his fifth album. "It wasn't that I didn't like it," he later observed. "I just had this feeling that we were treading water."

The biggest change was that bassist Ron Blair was no longer a member of the band. He had become increasingly unhappy about everything that goes along with being in a successful rock band, particularly the constant touring now that he was married. Tom himself conceded that being a Heartbreaker had become "a job." But Blair wanted more than a break; he wanted to get out of the music business entirely. His disinterest in the Heartbreakers had become all too obvious, making the call he received from manager Tony Dimitriades that it was time to move on not much of a surprise. So Blair left the rock world (for the moment), becoming the manager of a swimwear shop in Hermosa Beach.

He was around long enough to play bass on "Between Two Worlds," one of two songs (the other being "We Stand a Chance") recorded at RCA Studios on Sunset Boulevard, the same studio

Tom channels Pete Townshend. The *Long After Dark* tour began in September 1982 and ran through June 1983.

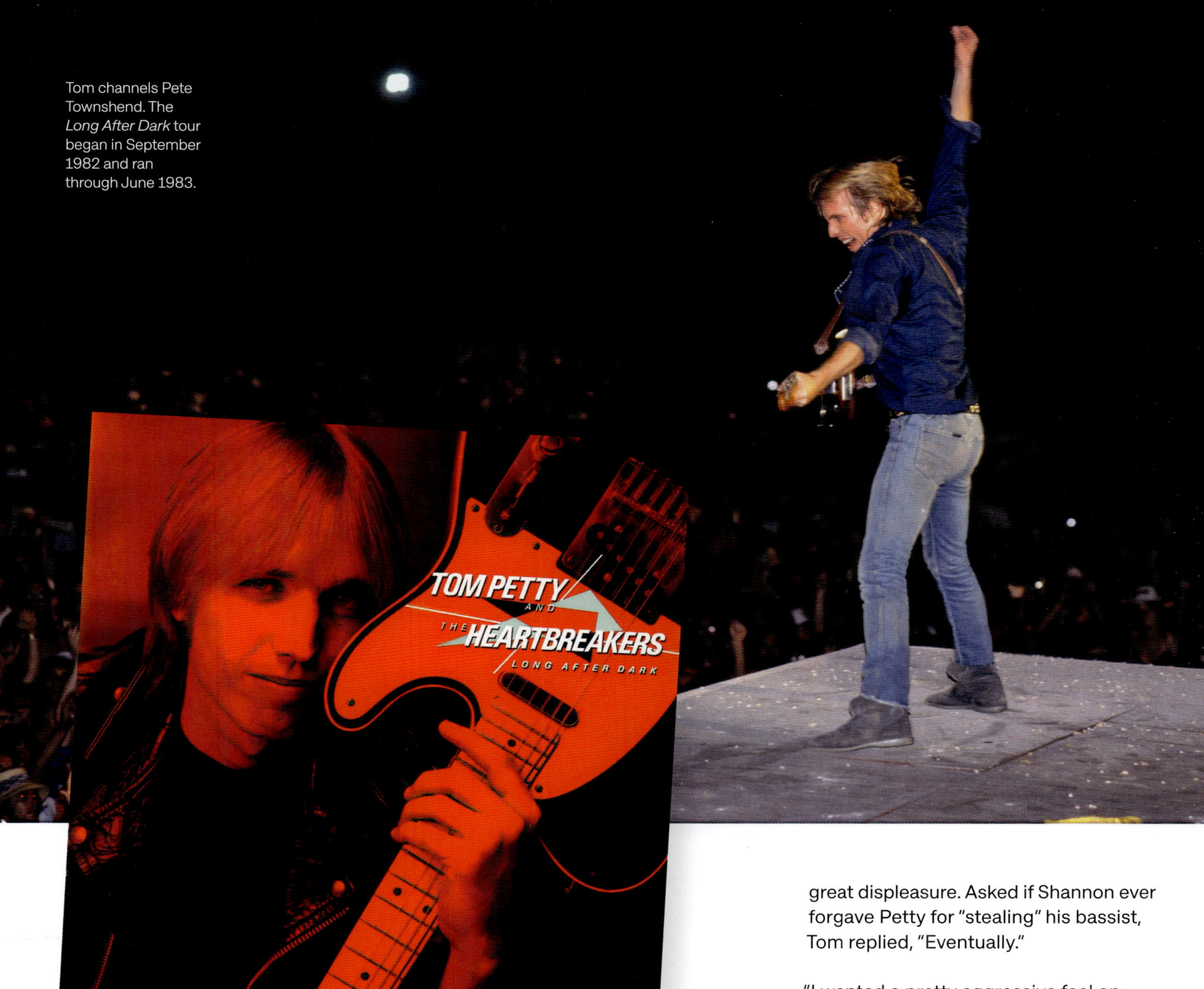

where the Rolling Stones had recorded "Satisfaction." The tracks had a "totally live" feel that Tom was pleased with. As he later told *Musician* about the album as a whole, "The sound on *Long After Dark* is more about the touring side of the band."

And the Heartbreakers soon found a new bassist in Howie Epstein, who was then playing with Del Shannon. Petty was producing Shannon's 1981 comeback album *Drop Down and Get Me* at the time, and he mentioned he was looking for a bassist for his own record. Shannon recommended Epstein, thinking Tom only wanted to use the bassist for recording. But Tom was looking for more than just a studio musician, and he asked Howie if he wanted to join his band permanently. Epstein quickly agreed, to Shannon's great displeasure. Asked if Shannon ever forgave Petty for "stealing" his bassist, Tom replied, "Eventually."

"I wanted a pretty aggressive feel on *Long After Dark*," Tom told *Hit Parader*. "I'm glad we did the softer things we did on *Hard Promises*, but that's out of my system now. I'm more interested in doing rock 'n' roll stuff, because I'm going to go on tour and I want to have a lot of rock 'n' roll songs to play." There were plenty of songs to choose from; the band recorded nineteen tracks, of which only ten made the final cut.

Side one in particular was a testament to the Heartbreakers' rededication to

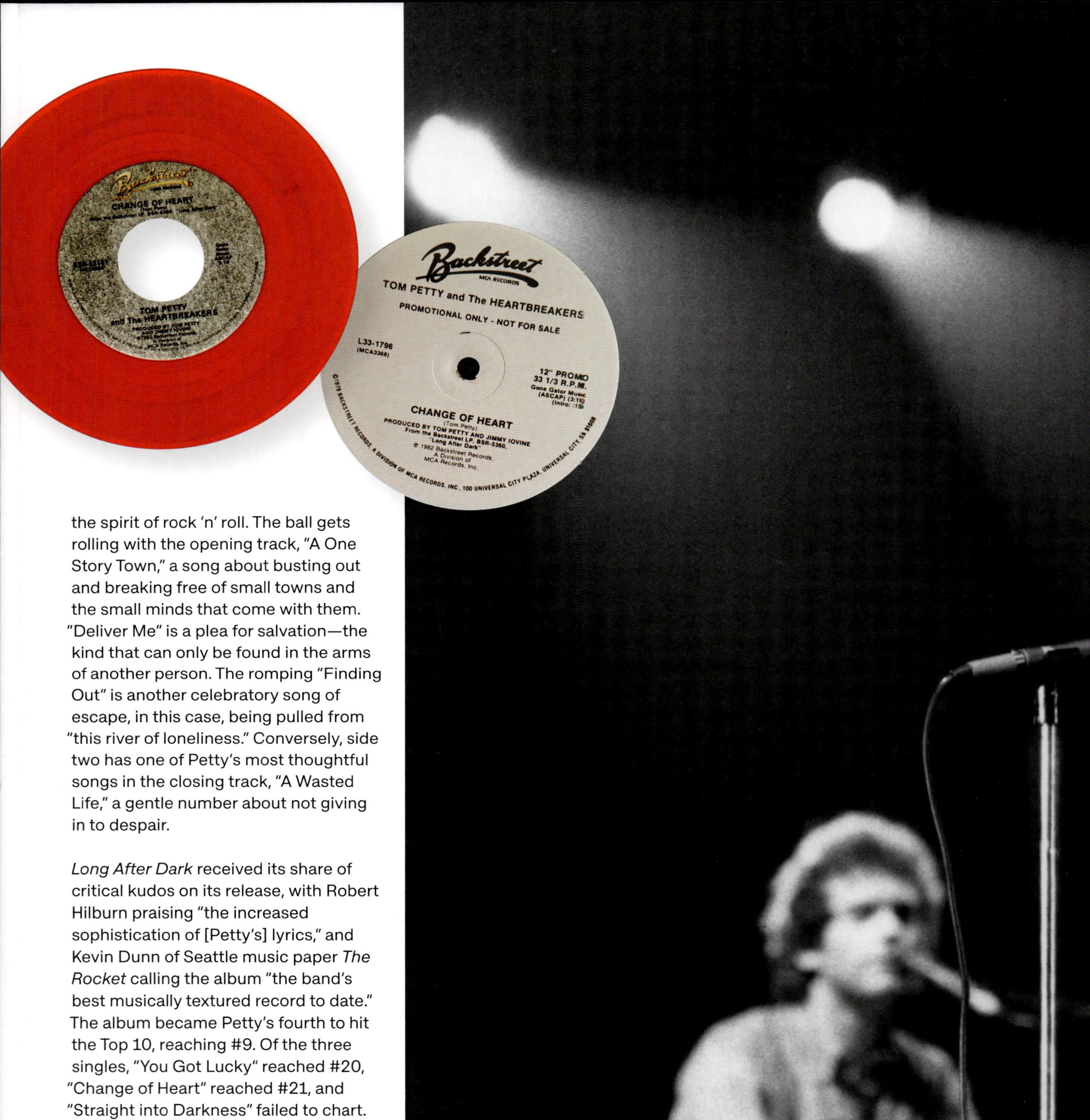

the spirit of rock 'n' roll. The ball gets rolling with the opening track, "A One Story Town," a song about busting out and breaking free of small towns and the small minds that come with them. "Deliver Me" is a plea for salvation—the kind that can only be found in the arms of another person. The romping "Finding Out" is another celebratory song of escape, in this case, being pulled from "this river of loneliness." Conversely, side two has one of Petty's most thoughtful songs in the closing track, "A Wasted Life," a gentle number about not giving in to despair.

Long After Dark received its share of critical kudos on its release, with Robert Hilburn praising "the increased sophistication of [Petty's] lyrics," and Kevin Dunn of Seattle music paper *The Rocket* calling the album "the band's best musically textured record to date." The album became Petty's fourth to hit the Top 10, reaching #9. Of the three singles, "You Got Lucky" reached #20, "Change of Heart" reached #21, and "Straight into Darkness" failed to chart. There would be a long three-year break before the Heartbreakers released another album.

The Heartbreakers in Paris on December 3, 1982. From left, Benmont Tench, Petty, and Mike Campbell.

23

THE LOST DOCUMENTARY

HEARTBREAKERS BEACH PARTY AND FRIENDSHIP WITH CAMERON CROWE

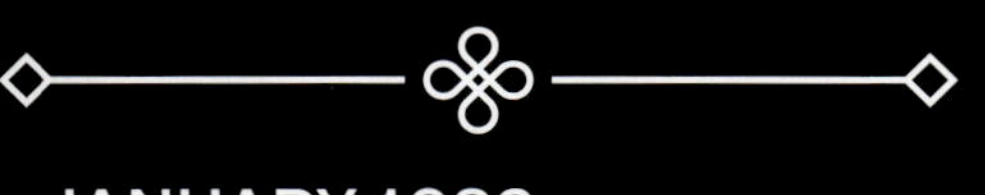

JANUARY 1983

Before award-winning filmmaker Cameron Crowe ascended to critical and commercial success with such films as *Jerry Maguire* and *Almost Famous*, he got his start with smaller projects—including the playful documentary *Heartbreakers Beach Party*.

Crowe was born and raised in California. An inveterate music fan, he began writing for the school newspaper as a teenager. A friendship with hallowed rock scribe Lester Bangs led to his writing for *Creem* (where Bangs was editor), as well as *Circus* and *Rolling Stone*—all before he'd turned eighteen. His 1981 book *Fast Times at Ridgemont High: A True Story* was based on his experiences posing as a high school senior at Clairemont High School in San Diego; he ended up writing the script for the 1982 film.

Crowe was a fan of Petty and the Heartbreakers, having first written about the band in *Rolling Stone*'s April 20, 1978, issue. Yet he never dreamed that a Heartbreakers project would bring him his first directorial credit. As he recalled to journalist Pamela Chelin, the life-changing moment came when Crowe was accompanying the band on their way to shoot the video for "You Got Lucky" when Petty told him, "Pick up a camera and I'll play you a song." "I said I wasn't a director," Crowe said. "He said, 'Just film me.' So I did. He played the novelty song 'I'm Stupid' and when it was done, he said, 'Guess what. Now you're a director.' Can't think of a better person to convince to jump in the deep end and start a new career."

Heartbreakers Beach Party is a mix of interviews, comedic segments (like Tom's rendition of "I'm Stupid," one of the film's highlights), and live footage; Crowe shares the director's credit with Doug Dowdle and Phil Savenick. Though at times satiric, there are also serious moments, as when Tom relates how frightening it was to be pulled off the stage during his December 30, 1978, performance at Winterland in San Francisco.

The film's title comes from a question Crowe asks about the band's reputation for being "road marauding banditos": "Has it changed much in the last few years or is it still pretty Heartbreakers beach party out there?" Petty allows he doesn't think "it'll ever change too much." He's later seen vamping through a song based around the phrase, dropping in references to 1960s-era dances like the Dog and the Swim, and announcing "Another modern classic!" at the end. The song would appear on the B-side of the "Change of Heart" single, released in early 1983.

The film aired on MTV—but only once. It was then pulled, reportedly over concerns about the bootlegged live footage, ironically turning the film itself into a prime target for bootleggers. The full one-hour-and-five-minute film was out of circulation for years, though clips from it did appear in such documentaries as *Runnin' Down a Dream* (2007). In 2024

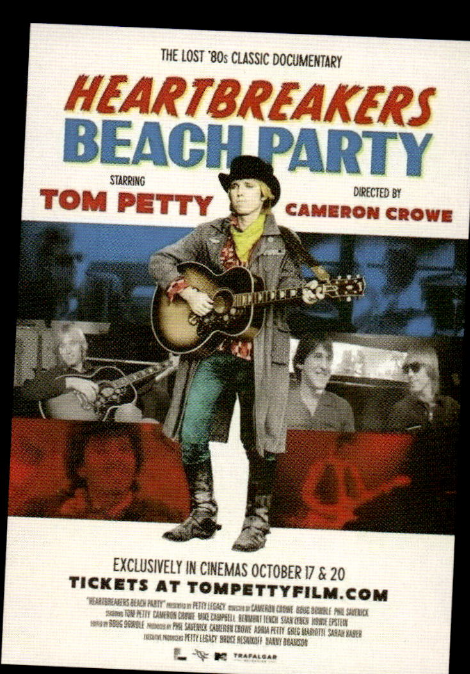

Heartbreakers Beach Party finally received a theatrical release in late 2024.

St. Petersburg beach party. Petty gave wunderkind rock scribe Cameron Crowe his directorial debut.

the film was given a brief theatrical run in select theaters around the United States.

Cameron and Tom ended up becoming friends, and Petty's songs often found their way into Crowe's films. Tom Cruise is seen singing "Free Fallin'" in *Jerry Maguire*. *Elizabethtown* features "Learning to Fly," a new mix of "It'll All Work Out," and the new songs "Square One" and "Jack." *We Bought a Zoo* featured "Don't Come Around Here No More." Crowe also would write the liner notes for the Heartbreakers' compilation *Anthology: Through the Years* (2000).

Amidst the live performance and rock 'n' roll banter, what comes through the most in the documentary is Tom's dedication to his career, his fans, and his craft. "At the risk of sounding corny, you have to thank the fans," he says at one point. "I'm still very reverent about that. I will stop and sign the thing because it's that important.

"All we can hope to do is inspire."

24

"THIS ONE TOOK THE CAKE"

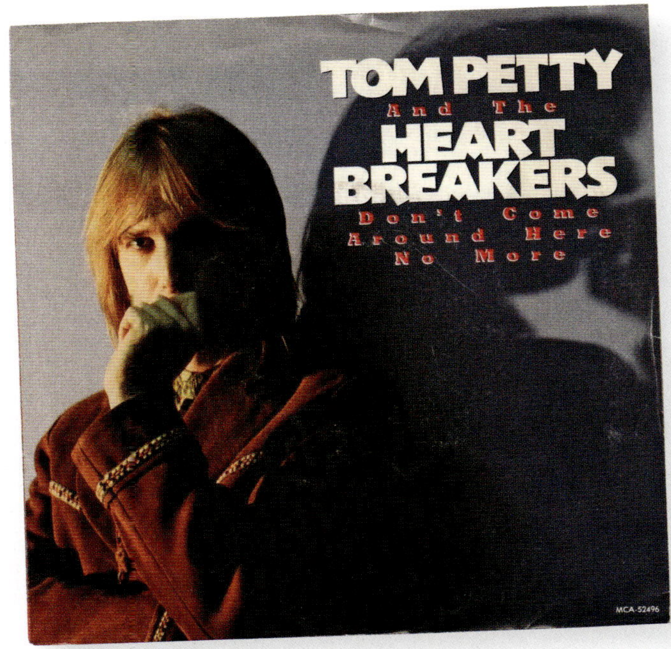

THE "DON'T COME AROUND HERE NO MORE" VIDEO

FEBRUARY 28, 1985

When people think of Tom Petty's videos, this creation, where Petty morphs into a psychedelicized Mad Hatter character, is what most likely comes to mind. Yet the song originally began as a prospective number for Stevie Nicks.

Jimmy Iovine, working on Stevie Nicks' *Rock a Little* album, had contacted Tom to see if he had any songs for her. Petty did not, but he suggested that Iovine contact Dave Stewart, one half of the synth-pop duo Eurythmics, whose songwriting Petty admired. Stewart had previously had his own encounter with Nicks, whom he'd met while on tour with his band, at a party at her home. He ended up staying the night, only to be thrown out the next morning. Stevie was still conflicted over her momentary split with Joe Walsh of the Eagles, and as she shoved him out the door, her parting words to Stewart were "Don't come around here no more!"

Instead of being stung by the rejection, Stewart began playing with the phrase. When he later met up with Iovine and played him a rough demo of the song, they decided to bring in Petty to help finish it, recording a basic track. When Stevie heard it, she was chagrined. It was a great song—but not one she felt she could bring anything else to. "I just looked at them and said, 'I'm going to top that? Really?' I got up, thanked Dave, thanked Tom, fired Jimmy, and left. That went down in about five minutes."

So the song ended up with the Heartbreakers. And though Stewart has said the *Alice in Wonderland* theme of the video was his concept, reflecting his experiences in the "wonderland" of Los Angeles, the video's director, Jeff Stein, told *Yahoo! Entertainment* that the idea was his, inspired by Tom's penchant for wearing top hats. Stein wasn't sure how receptive Petty would be for the idea, thinking of him as a "straight-ahead rocker" who "wouldn't be that adventurous." But Tom loved the idea: "He really went for it," said Stein.

The video's environment is one that will resonate with anyone familiar with Lewis Carroll's *Alice* books. A wide-eyed Alice, played by Louise Foley, is offered a bite of magic mushroom by a sinister, hookah-smoking Stewart, who sports fiendishly long fingernails. Tom is the smirking

Mad Hatter, who serves Alice a cup of tea that changes in size, until she finds herself floating helplessly in it.

In the most disturbing sequence, Alice is transformed into a life-sized cake, with Tom and his minions taking great delight in slicing her into pieces and devouring her; the cake's spurting strawberry filling even makes the proceedings look something like a slasher film. Editing toned down that aspect for the final cut, but MTV still felt the sequence was too "lascivious" and asked for another cut. "It was just a shot of me grinning," Tom told *Billboard*, "and they were like 'Well, you can do it, but you can't enjoy it *that* much.'"

There were still complaints about the sequence when the video was released, inspiring Tipper Gore to join forces with other outraged parents in forming the Parents Music Resource Center, pushing back against what they felt was excessive violence and sexual content in popular music. "I was cited for promoting cannibalism by a parents/teachers group," Stein said. "I thought, 'Well this *has* to be a career high, if you can bring back cannibalism as a fad!'" The single reached #13, while the video was nominated for four MTV Music Video Awards: Video of the Year, Best Direction, Viewer's Choice, and Best Special Effects, winning in the latter category. It remained one of Tom's favorite videos. As he recalled in *I Want My MTV*, "I was knocked out when I saw the final cut. I played it 30 times in a row."

Tom's penchant for top hats made him a natural "Mad Hatter" in the "Don't Come Around Here No More" video.

25

“TOM PETTY’S REBEL YELL”

SOUTHERN ACCENTS

MARCH 26, 1985

On stage in Hoffman Estates, Illinois, on June 20, 1987.

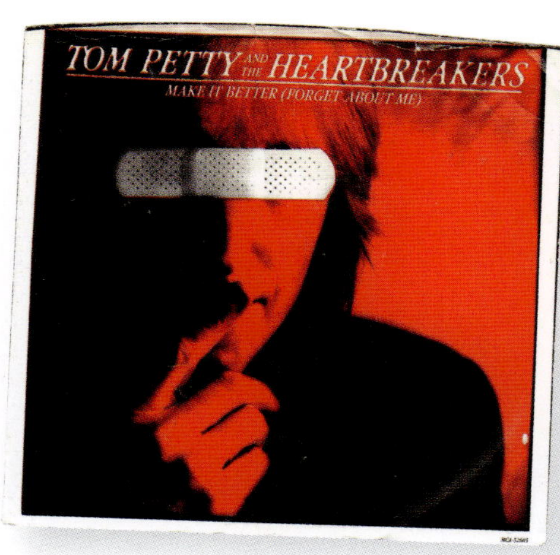

It was the album that sounded unlike any record the Heartbreakers had released before. It was also the album that almost ended Tom's career as a musician.

While on the tour promoting *Long After Dark*, Tom decided he wanted to make an album reflecting his Southern roots. He even considered recording in Florida, but realized it would be too expensive.

The sessions began with the band working for the first time without a producer; Tom and Mike Campbell would take on that role themselves. And to make things more comfortable, recording would be held at the studio he had built in his home, christened Gone Gator One. As it turned out, things became a little too comfortable. Outsiders dropped by and drugs and alcohol added to the party atmosphere. As Petty confessed to biographer Warren Zanes, when he listened to the album, "I can taste cocaine in the back of my mouth"; you can practically see him shuddering at the memory.

The arrival of Dave Stewart, who cowrote three of the album's tracks, also took the record away from its Southern theme, with songs like "Trailer" being cut in favor of Stewart's songs. Then there were the recordings themselves, which Tom felt didn't sound nearly as good as the demos. One day, as he listened to yet another mix of "Rebels," he punched the wall in frustration and ended up shattering every bone in his left hand. There were varying accounts given as to why Petty hit the wall, but the end result was the same: his hand was severely damaged, and doctors told him he might never play the guitar again.

Surgery and months of therapy followed, as Tom fought his way back to being able to play guitar. But the incident also served as a wake-up call. Jimmy Iovine was brought in to restore some order, and recording moved to a new studio, Village Recorders. The planned double album was cut to a single disc. There ended up being all kinds of new sounds on the album. Drum machines. Horns. A Coral guitar, which makes a sitar-like sound (played by Dave Stewart). A string arrangement by musician/producer Jack Nitzsche, best known for his work with the Rolling Stones and Neil Young. But in the midst of all the newfound diversity, the title track speaks to the album's initial inspiration, a meditation on one's own cultural history.

MCA hired Jon Scott, who was responsible for getting the Heartbreakers their first chart success, to help launch the album. Scott suggested having a private listening party for the industry representatives who would be in LA for the annual *Radio & Records* convention (*Radio & Records* was a music industry trade magazine). Scott jokingly added that the party should be held at Petty's house and was surprised when Tom agreed. True to his word, on the night of the party, Tom was at the door to greet each guest as they arrived, personally handing a chilled glass of Dom Pérignon to everyone.

Southern Accents landed in the Top 10, reaching #7. In addition to "Don't Come Around Here No More," two other tracks were released as singles, "Rebels," which only reached #74 in *Billboard*'s main chart but hit #5 in the Mainstream Rock Tracks chart, and "Make It Better (Forget About Me)," which reached #54 in the main chart and #12 in the Mainstream Rock Tracks chart.

The album continues to generate a diverse response. At the time of its release, the *Melbourne Age* stated, "There is no doubt that this will go down as one of the best albums of 1985." But in *Tom Petty: Every Album, Every Song*, author Richard James calls it "a confused, incoherent, and frustrating collection." Tom himself was unhappy with some elements, saying of "Rebels," "I don't think the vocal's that good on it."

“WE KILLED IT”

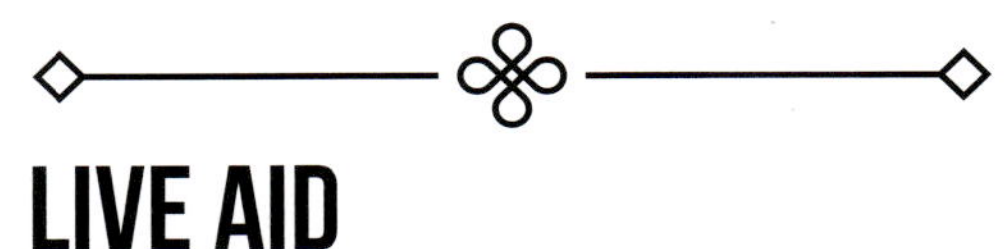

LIVE AID

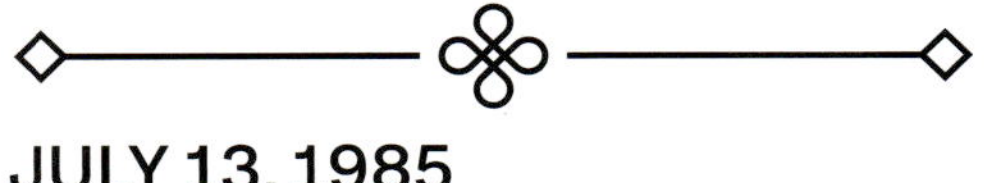

JULY 13, 1985

Now firmly a part of the rock establishment, Tom was a natural choice to appear at the Live Aid benefit concerts.

The genesis of Live Aid dated back to the 1984 release of the UK charity single “Do They Know It’s Christmas?” which raised funds for African famine relief. The project was spearheaded by Boomtown Rats lead singer Bob Geldof, who cowrote the song with Midge Ure, then brought together a supergroup of performers (including George Michael, Sting, and Bono) who recorded the single under the joint name Band Aid. The Americans responded with the charity single “We Are the World,” released in 1985 and featuring Michael Jackson (who cowrote the song with Lionel Richie), Tina Turner, and Bruce Springsteen, among others. Then the idea of holding a charity concert was born. In the end, there were two, one held at Wembley Stadium in London and another at John F. Kennedy Stadium in Philadelphia.

In the summer of 1985, Petty and the Heartbreakers were on tour promoting the *Southern Accents* album. On July 12, the band had just played a successful show at the USF Sun Dome in Tampa, Florida, and were relaxing in their dressing room. Then, according to Jimmy Zavala (a.k.a. “Jimmy Z”), who was playing saxophone and harmonica in the band, the band’s manager, Tony Dimitriades,

The Live Aid performance put the Heartbreakers in front of a worldwide audience.

surprised them by coming in and telling everyone they had to pack their bags; they were leaving that night to fly to Philly and "to play a concert the next day called Live Aid."

In a post on his blog, Zavala recalled the flight north being enlivened "thanks to party favors I'd scored and a bottle of Courvoisier." On arrival in Philadelphia at 6 a.m., the band had a few hours to rest at their hotel before heading to the stadium. In his suite, Zavala switched on the television just in time to catch an interview with Phil Collins, who had just played the Live Aid event in the UK and was about to board the Concorde to play a second set at the US event. When the coverage then cut to the thousands of fans at JFK Stadium, Zavala realized "OMG—we're into something big today."

At the stadium, Zavala recalled the weather "hot as hell and humid." The band was scheduled to go on at 5 p.m., sandwiched between sets by Madonna and Kenny Loggins. Given that they'd be facing a worldwide audience, the band was understandably nervous, but Neil Young gave them a little last-minute support, as they ascended the stairs to the stage. "He smiled and said something like 'Knock 'em dead boys,'" Zavala recalled. "And we did."

The Live Aid sets were short; the Heartbreakers had time to play four songs. As the curtains opened, the band launched into a lively "American Girl," Tom in a black jacket decorated with stars, moons, and the planet Saturn, and wearing 1960s-era Byrds-style sunglasses. "How are ya?" he called out after the song, then went into "The Waiting," the crowd joining in on the "yeah yeah" passages. Without a pause, the band continued with "Rebels," and then wrapped up the set with a powerful "Refugee," Tom holding his guitar up in triumph at the end.

Despite the brevity of the set, the band definitely made an impression. Their set was singled out for praise by *New York Times* critic Robert Palmer, who wrote, "Some of the most riveting moments came from relatively unsung instrumentalists, many of them mere sidemen to the stars. The guitarist Mike Campbell and pianist Benmont Trench of Tom Petty and the Heartbreakers proved their mettle as two of the strongest, most resourceful team players in rock."

And then the band headed off to get to their show the next night in Wantagh, New York.

27

BONDING WITH BOB

The Heartbreakers' performance with Dylan at Farm Aid would very soon lead to bigger things.

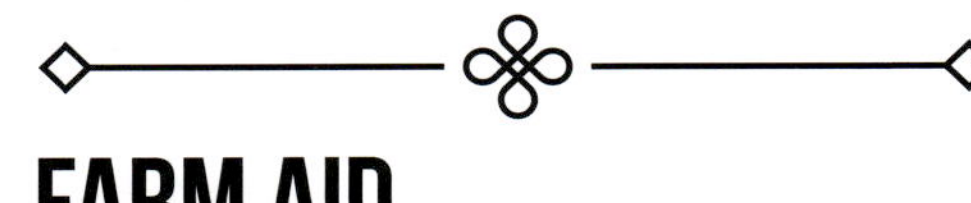

FARM AID

SEPTEMBER 22, 1985

When the Heartbreakers backed Bob Dylan during his surprise performance at Farm Aid, it was the first step in a lasting bond that would develop between Petty and Dylan.

During Dylan's three-song set at Live Aid, he made what some thought were ill-considered comments: "I hope that some of the money that's raised for the people of Africa, maybe they can just take a little bit of it, one or two million, maybe, and use it, say, to pay the mortgages on some of the farms that the farmers here owe to the banks." Live Aid organizer Bob Geldof called the remarks "crass, stupid and nationalistic"; after all, the event wasn't about American concerns.

But they struck a chord with country musician Willie Nelson, who decided that providing aid to US farmers was a cause worthy of its own benefit. Nelson, along with musicians Neil Young and John Mellencamp, quickly organized a benefit concert they called Farm Aid, held in Champaign, Illinois. As the unwitting instigator of the event, Bob Dylan was asked to participate, and Petty and the Heartbreakers were tapped to join him.

Dylan and Petty had crossed paths before. While attending Dylan's June 7, 1978, concert at the Universal Amphitheatre in LA, Petty was startled to hear Dylan introduce him from the stage, after he'd pointed out that Joni Mitchell was in attendance: "And Tom Petty is here. He's a new rising star." After the show, he was invited backstage for a brief meeting with Bob. He later shared a bill with Dylan at the Peace Sunday concert, held at the Rose Bowl in Pasadena, California, on June 6, 1982, when Petty performed two Buddy Holly songs, "Not Fade Away" and "Well . . . All Right," as part of a trio with Jackson Browne and Gary U. S. Bonds.

In contrast to his Live Aid performance, when he, Keith Richards, and Ron Wood had all played acoustic guitars, Dylan wanted a full electric band behind him at Farm Aid. Dylan's manager, Elliot Roberts, also handled the Heartbreakers and suggested they would work well together; Heartbreakers keyboardist Benmont Tench had also previously played on Dylan's records. Petty was quick to agree, excited to work with a musician he much admired.

"We spent a week rehearsing," he recalled to *Rolling Stone*, "and we would play a lot every night. Hours and hours and hours. We did Hank Williams songs, Motown songs; 'I Second That Emotion.' We even played 'Louie Louie' one night. And 'Then He Kissed Me,' the old Crystals song." Elsewhere in the article he noted, "I think Bob's attracted to the idea of working with a group. A handpicked band of good players doesn't always make a great band. Somebody like him needs a sympathetic unit that understands that music. He told me, 'This band is like talking to one guy.'"

From the moment the Dylan/Heartbreakers kicked off their set, it was obvious how comfortable the musicians were with each other, not to mention how much fun they were having. And the song choices mixed things up nicely. The opener, "Clean-Cut Kid," was making its live debut. The band got into a smooth groove with a cover of Sam Cooke's "Shake," followed by two more live debuts: "I'll Remember You" and "Trust Yourself" (all the live debuts were from Dylan's *Empire Burlesque* album). The most unusual song in the set was the dreamy, sentimental "That Lucky Old Sun," a 1949 song that was a big hit for Frankie Laine. The set wrapped up with a rousing "Maggie's Farm."

The only bad thing anyone could find to say about the performance was that it was too short: "Everyone was saying, 'Boy, it's a shame we can't really play for a while,'" Petty recalled. But the opportunity to do so was just around the corner.

Tom backstage with Bob Dylan at the first Farm Aid, September 22, 1985, Champaign, Illinois.

"HE'S LIKE A STOIC BIG BROTHER"

TOURING WITH BOB DYLAN

FEBRUARY 5, 1986

The Heartbreakers had just finished their Farm Aid set with Bob Dylan and were hanging out in their trailer when Bob stopped by with a question: "Hey, what would you think of doing a tour? I've got a tour of Australia I want to do, and what would you guys think of doing that?" And just like that, the Heartbreakers were adopted as Dylan's new backing band.

The band had thought of Farm Aid as a one-off. They were busy gearing up to work on their next album. But this seemed like too good an opportunity to pass up. Initially, the True Confessions tour only encompassed Pacific Rim countries: New Zealand, Australia, and Japan. But excitement about the double act meant that a US leg was soon added. So it was back into more intensive rehearsals, as the band worked their way through Dylan's impressive catalogue. But Tom also found the work "inspiring." Dylan liked to mix it up, not even having a confirmed setlist for each show, and he also reworked older songs into new arrangements. "It's a little like playing with a jazz artist," Petty told biographer Paul Zollo. "They improvise."

Tom soon found himself collaborating with Dylan as well, co-writing lyrics for Mike Campbell's "Jammin' Me" (which would appear on the Heartbreakers' *Let Me Up [I've Had Enough]* album), and "Got My Mind Made Up" (recorded with the Heartbreakers and released on Dylan's *Knocked Out Loaded* album). While in Australia, the Heartbreakers and Bob also recorded the song "Band of the Hand," for the film of the same name.

The tour got off to a rocky start. When the band's sound check at the open-air venue for their first date in Wellington, New Zealand, proved to be too loud for the area's residents, the show was nearly cancelled. It was eventually allowed to go on as scheduled, followed by a post-show celebration at the Park Royal Hotel's bar. Benmont Tench took over on piano, sparking a singalong of such R&B classics as "Save the Last Dance for Me" and "Poison Ivy," with a little help from Stevie Nicks, who had come down under to see the show.

When the tour hit the states, there was a preview of what was to come when Dylan and the Heartbreakers played a short set at Amnesty International's "A Conspiracy of Hope" show in LA on June 6. The first full US show came on June 9 in San Diego, with the US leg running through August 6. *Desert Sun* reviewer Eleni P. Austin called the Heartbreakers "the best outfit Dylan has had with him since the Band." The *Chicago Tribune*'s Jonathan Taylor noted how Petty "seemed to revel in not having to be in the spotlight. He joined Dylan at the microphone to share vocals several times, but, more often, he simply looked like an artist who was thrilled to be playing with one of his major influences."

A typical set alternated between full band sequences with Dylan, the Heartbreakers taking over for some numbers ("Refugee"

Petty found Dylan's tendency to work without a setlist and improvise new arrangements onstage inspiring.

was frequently cited as a highlight), and solo acoustic spots from Dylan. The tour was documented in the concert film *Hard to Handle*, by acclaimed Australian director Gillian Armstrong. The following year, Dylan took the Heartbreakers on the road again for the Temple of Flames tour, which began on September 5 in Tel-Aviv, Israel, then toured Europe before closing in London on October 17, 1987. It was after a show in Birmingham during the UK leg that Tom first met Jeff Lynne, with whom he'd soon be working extensively.

Petty would remain good friends with Dylan for the rest of his life. "I was lucky to be around him," he said. "I never took it for granted that I was getting to work with someone who was a master of what he was doing."

Petty soon was collaborating with Dylan offstage as well, co-writing lyrics for Mike Campbell's "Jammin' Me."

The Heartbreakers 1986 and 1987 tours with Bob Dylan took them around the US, over to the UK and Europe, down under to Australia, and also to Japan.

"A GOOD ROCK AND ROLL ALBUM"

LET ME UP (I'VE HAD ENOUGH)

APRIL 21, 1987

Maybe the Heartbreakers just started getting restless if they didn't have enough to do. But instead of relaxing when they'd completed the first leg of the Bob Dylan True Confessions tour in 1986, the band headed right back into the studio to make their seventh album.

It ended up being, as Tom described it, "kind of a mongrel" of an album. There was no involvement from Jimmy Iovine; Tom coproduced with Mike Campbell. It was the first studio album without a contribution from Rob Blair (who'd appeared on one track of *Southern Accents*). In fact, there were no other outside musicians at all—no horns, no additional percussion, no backing vocalists. And, as Tom explained to *Rolling Stone*, "The only rule of the sessions was the tape had to roll from the time the first guy got here until the last guy was gone."

It meant that *Let Me Up* would have a loose, improvisational feel. It wasn't unusual for Tom to call out the chord changes as the band worked their way through a new song, pulling it together on the fly. "The Damage You've Done," for example, was "ad-libbed completely," according to Tom, the band first recording a country version (which can be found on the *Playback* box set), then going in a more rock direction on the second take, which was used on the final album.

The album's outstanding track "Jammin' Me," a cheeky rocker, was the opening track and the first single. The song was crafted from a demo by Campbell. Petty then cowrote lyrics with Bob Dylan during a writing session at LA's Sunset Marquis hotel, then rewrote the music with Campbell ("We changed the melody and the chord structure somewhat"). It's a song of frustration, a push back at being painted into a corner. Eventually the grievances go beyond the personal, the narrator telling his adversary to take back any number of things causing problems: acid rain, pension plans, El Salvador,

Tom enjoys a quiet moment in Hollywood, California, in 1987. *Let Me Up* was the first Heartbreakers album in a while that featured no outside musicians.

Powering through a set at Pine Knob Music Theater in Clarkson, Michigan, on June 18, 1987.

Brothers in arms: Tom with Mike Campbell, the Heartbreaker he relied on more than any other band member.

and Apple computers. One verse became notorious for its singling out a few celebrities: Vanessa Redgrave, Joe Piscopo, and Eddie Murphy.

It was an album of contrasts. There's the delicacy of a mandolin and Japanese koto providing a graceful touch on "It'll All Work Out." The rollicking good run of "Think About Me," another ad-libbed track. The slinky, cynical "My Life/Your World" has an irresistible charm. And the title track serves as a raw homage to the Rolling Stones.

Let Me Up reached #20 on its release, but it was seen as something of a disappointment. *Southern Accents* had hit the Top 10 and was certified platinum; *Let Me Up* was only certified gold. It nonetheless got good reviews. Robert Hilburn, the band's longtime supporter at the *Los Angeles Times* called the album "the group's liveliest and most assured work since *Damn the Torpedoes*. . . . Petty writes with a richness and detail that reaffirm his place among rock's most prized songwriters."

As for the singles, "Jammin' Me" reached #18 and topped *Billboard*'s Mainstream Rock Tracks chart. The song sparked a minor controversy when Eddie Murphy made his displeasure about being named in the song clear; Petty recalled watching Murphy on TV being "really pissed off about it" (Tom viewed the lyrics as an attack on celebrity culture in general, not the specific personalities). Subsequent singles, the melancholy "Runaway Trains" and the synth-heavy "All Mixed Up," didn't chart in the Hot 100, but they reached #6 and #19, respectively, in the Mainstream Rock Tracks chart.

After the more elaborate production on their previous album, *Let Me Up* offered the Heartbreakers a chance to get back to basics and reestablish their own identity after serving as someone else's backing band. As Tom put it, "This was very much a group album."

30

UP IN SMOKE

Nine days after he lost nearly everything in the house fire, Tom was back on tour.

THE HOME INFERNO

MAY 17, 1987

It was supposed to be a day of celebration. Then it became a disaster—and could've easily become a tragedy.

It was the birthday of Tom's first wife, Jane, and there were plans for a party to be held that afternoon. But while having breakfast at their home, the family detected the telltale scent of smoke, followed by the frightening realization that their house was on fire. Tom was able to get his wife and younger daughter Annakim (daughter Adria had stayed overnight at a friend's), outside, then tried fighting the blaze along with the housekeeper until the firefighters arrived. But the fire had spread quickly; when he picked up a hose, it melted in his hands. Thankfully, there were minimal injuries. The only person hurt was the housekeeper, who ended up with some minor burns. But it was nonetheless a traumatizing experience to go through.

The house was nearly completely destroyed, with one key exception. Tom's home studio, Gone Gator One, was mostly spared, as were the instruments and recordings he had stored there, which could be salvaged. It was some consolation. In the immediate aftermath of the fire, Eurythmics singer Annie Lennox, who was both a friend and a neighbor, arrived to help, buying the family clothes and taking them to a nearby hotel.

It was even more disturbing to learn later that the fire was not an accident, like Tom had assumed, or due to something like faulty wiring, but had been deliberately set. It was arson. Tom's stunned reaction was, "Who'd want to kill me?" But investigators detected evidence indicating someone had tried. They deduced that the arsonist had cut a hole in the back fence and had been watching the house for some time, then poured lighter fluid on a back staircase and set it alight.

Tom's family was fortunate to survive the fire that consumed their home.

The family was soon able to escape the horror. The Heartbreakers had an upcoming tour set to begin on May 26, what was billed as the Rock 'n' Roll Caravan '87 tour, with the Georgia Satellites and the Del Fuegos also on the bill. The Pettys were glad to get away, though thoughts of the fire were never far away. "I had kind of a weird week last week," Tom told the crowd during the tour's second show, at Arizona State University in Tempe. "Somebody came and burned my house to the ground." Then he put a positive spin on the situation, holding up his Rickenbacker while saying, "But it's all right, really—they didn't burn this."

Petty had a new home rebuilt on the same site. But he still was shaken by the event. He later said he wouldn't use the word "fire" in a song (ironically, his next tour with Bob Dylan was named the Temple in Flames tour). And as he told journalist Jaan Uhelszki, he didn't want to write any "vicious and angry" songs for a while; "I didn't want to do anything except sing really light, happy music after that." He felt that attitude ultimately took him to a better place: "I think knowing someone was maybe trying to kill me revitalized me. I came out of it in a good spot. It just made me glad to be alive." Some have suggested that the defiant sentiments of "I Won't Back Down" (which appeared on 1989's *Full Moon Fever*) were directed toward the arsonist, but Petty himself never confirmed that in any interview.

When it was announced that the fire was arson, a number of people falsely confessed to the crime (a phenomenon that is not unusual). But the real culprit was never found, and the crime remains unsolved to this day.

PART 3

IT'S GOOD TO BE KING, 1987–1996

Tom leads the Heartbreakers through a set at New York City's Madison Square Garden, July 8, 1987.

31

ACTING NATURALLY

Tom as the laconic mayor of "Bridge City" in the postapocalyptic film *The Postman*.

PETTY ONSCREEN

NOVEMBER 6, 1987

It's just another day on *It's Garry Shandling's Show*. Garry's friends Pete and Jackie Schumaker have come by, Jackie on the verge of giving birth, an experience she wants to share on Garry's program. But when the child declines to arrive on command, some diversion is needed. Help arrives when there's a knock on the door, which Garry rushes to answer. Then comes the unexpected announcement: "Hey everybody! It's Tom Petty!"

"I just wanted to return the hedge clippers," Tom says, clippers in hand, adding, "My yard looks great!" But you're not going to let Tom Petty drop by without doing a song, especially since his guitar is conveniently slung over his shoulder. And so he takes center stage to perform "The Waiting." Tom made four appearances on Shandling's show in 1987 and 1989 (the two were good friends and for a time lived across the street from each other), part of a small but not insignificant aspect of his career—his work in television and film.

Tom's first film appearance was in *FM* (1978), a comedy about life at an FM rock station, playing himself. Tom dismissed the film as a "beach party radio movie," but the soundtrack, which featured the Heartbreakers' "Breakdown," did go platinum.

He spent the next decade limiting his time before the cameras to music videos. But in 1987 he turned up in a small role in *Made in Heaven*, playing a bar patron who is robbed while playing

Tom made a number of appearances on *The Gerry Shandling Show*; at one time, he was Shandling's real-life neighbor.

dice. He's remarkably laconic about the experience. When Timothy Hutton, one of the thieves, refers to him by the wrong name, "Stinky," Petty's quick to correct him—"Stanky"—but doesn't make any attempt to hold on to his cash.

He's equally low key in *The Postman*, a 1997 epic about a postapocalyptic world, starring Kevin Costner. Costner, who also directed the film, had asked Petty to play the part of the mayor of Bridge City. "And it was at a time when I really needed to do something," Tom told *Rolling Stone*. "I was, like, lost. The band had stopped touring. I lived alone. I needed to do something with my time, and this sounded perfect, so I took off and went up to Washington [state], in the middle of the woods somewhere, bald eagles going over and freezing cold in July." When Costner's character, the titular postman, rides into Bridge City, he regards Petty with curiosity for a moment before saying, "I know you. You're famous." Completing the in-joke, Petty responds, "I was once."

Tom also made an appearance on Shandling's subsequent program, *The Larry Sanders Show*, the same year. And there was also an obligatory appearance on the animated series *The Simpsons* in the 2002 episode "How I Spent My Strummer Vacation," with Homer attending a rock 'n' roll fantasy camp, where he meets Tom's earnest suggestions of how to improve one's lyric writing with a staunch *"Boring!"*

Then came his longest running role, voicing the character of Elroy "Lucky" Kleinschmidt on the animated series *King of the Hill* from 2004 to 2009. Tom was introduced to the show by actor Billy Bob Thornton, who had told him "Man, you're just going to love this" (Thornton had previously offered Petty a part in his 2001 film *Daddy and Them*, but recording commitments kept Tom from accepting). Series creator Mike Judge explained that Lucky had been conceived as looking "like Tom Petty without the success. And we thought, what if we tried to get Tom Petty?" Tom was happy to accept and did so well the character was brought back for a total of twenty-nine episodes.

But however much he enjoyed acting, music remained his main gig. "I don't want to be a musician that turns into an actor," Tom told SFX Radio in 1999. "It's just something to do if there's nothing else to do. It's kind of fun and I like film a lot, so I get to learn and hang around."

Petty co-starred alongside several fellow rockers in an episode of *The Simpsons* that first aired in November 2002. From left, Elvis Costello, Petty, Keith Richards, Homer Simpson, Mick Jagger, Lenny Kravitz, and Brian Setzer.

32

"THERE WAS NEVER EVEN A GLIMPSE OF EGO"

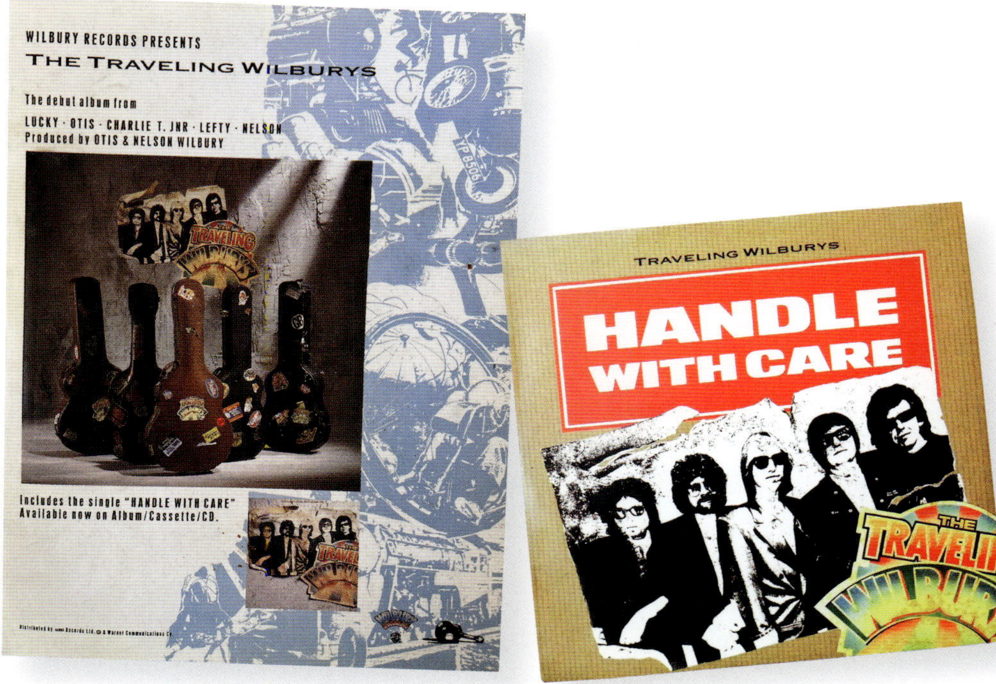

THE FICTITIOUS SUPERGROUP

APRIL 5, 1988

If you'd told a thirteen-year-old Tom Petty, as he watched the Beatles perform on *The Ed Sullivan Show* in February 1964, that one day he'd be playing in a group with the band's guitarist, George Harrison, he wouldn't have believed you. But that's exactly what ended up happening.

Though the Traveling Wilburys seemed to come together purely by chance, it was a concept Harrison had been mulling over for some time. While working on his 1987 album *Cloud Nine*, he brought up the idea with his producer (and former Electric Light Orchestra founder) Jeff Lynne, while the two were kicking back over a couple of beers. "A group? Who should we have in it then?" Lynne asked. "Bob Dylan," was Harrison's reply. Other names surfaced: Roy Orbison, whom Harrison had first met when the Beatles toured with him back in 1963; Tom Petty, whom Harrison had encountered over the years since they first met at Leon Russell's home in LA back in 1974. For Lynne, it was a "pipe dream" conversation. But it was a dream that ended up coming true.

When "This Is Love" was chosen as *Cloud Nine*'s third single, Harrison decided to add a new song to the 12-inch and CD versions of the release. He and Lynne, both in Los Angeles at the time, planned to put the track together quickly. Dylan became a part of the project when Harrison and Lynne asked if they could record at his home studio. Lynne had been working with Orbison on his *Mystery Girl* album, making him an obvious candidate. And Harrison had recently left his guitar at Petty's house, so on picking it up it was natural to extend an invite to him as well; it didn't hurt that Lynne was also working with Petty on his *Full Moon Fever* album.

Everyone gathered at Dylan's place in Malibu on April 5, 1988. Harrison and Lynne had the song partially roughed out. The five musicians quickly completed the backing track, wrote the lyrics during their dinner break, and had the number finished in about five hours. The title, "Handle With Care," was taken from a packing crate in the garage.

The Traveling Wilburys brought together five stellar talents; the fun they had working together was obvious.

When Warner Brothers president Mo Ostin heard the song, he quickly realized its potential. Instead of burying it as a B-side, he suggested the musicians continue recording until they had enough for an album. Harrison readily agreed, and sessions were set up the following month at Dave Stewart's LA home studio, from May 7 to 16. Final overdubs were done at Harrison's home studio in England.

Echoing the premise of *Sgt. Pepper's Lonely Hearts Club Band*, where the Beatles adopted the guise of a psychedelic troupe of players, Harrison's impromptu group created a new persona for itself: the Traveling Wilburys. Running with the concept, each member of the band took on a pseudonym: Nelson (Harrison), Otis (Lynne), Lucky (Dylan), Charlie T. Jr. (Petty), and Lefty (Orbison). The original album cover kept the joke going; none of the musicians' real names appear in the credits.

Traveling Wilburys Vol. 1 was released in 1988 and was an instant success, hitting the Top 10 in nine countries, including the US. It would go on to win the Grammy for Best Rock Performance by a Duo or Group with Vocal. Sadly, Orbison died on December 6, 1988, at the age of fifty-two. But little over a year later, the remaining Wilburys recorded songs for a second album, which they mischievously titled *Traveling Wilburys Vol. 3*. They also took on new pseudonyms: Spike (Harrison), Clayton (Lynne), Muddy (Petty), and Boo (Dylan) and dedicated the album to the departed Lefty Wilbury. The album was released in 1990.

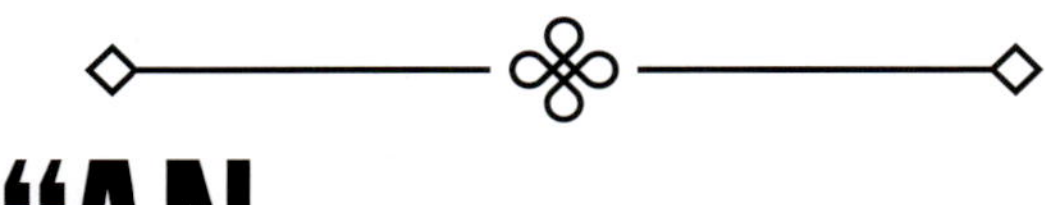

"AN UNEXPECTED TREAT"

THE TRAVELING WILBURYS ALBUMS

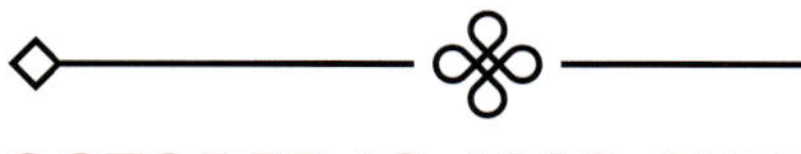

OCTOBER 18, 1988, AND OCTOBER 29, 1990

The rock world has seen any number of supergroups—Cream, Audioslave, Them Crooked Vultures. What made the Traveling Wilburys records different was the light-hearted approach. With both albums, you get a sense of hanging out with a group of friends at a backyard party who are jamming together, having fun, and taking delight in each other's company.

Those good spirits are immediately evident in "Handle With Care," the lead-off track on *Traveling Wilburys Vol. 1* and the album's first single. The loping song is a sweet plea to a new love, with the singer admitting to his vulnerability and asking that he be treated gently. George Harrison takes the first lead vocal, but it's when Roy Orbison comes in, singing of how tired he is of being on his own, that you understand why the other Wilburys were so anxious to get him in the group. They had grown up hearing his dulcet voice in such classics as "Only the Lonely," "Crying," and "In Dreams." It was a sound that would add a touch of melancholy to the Wilburys' work, even in the ostensibly optimistic "Not Alone Any More."

Elsewhere, "Rattled" is jumped up rockabilly, Bob Dylan growls his way through the wordplay of "Tweeter and the Monkey Man," and the ska lilt of "Last Night" sees Tom ruefully jousting with a predatory woman. As Bill DeYoung wrote in the *Gainesville Sun*, "Unassuming and unpretentious, the Traveling Wilburys' album is the kind of record the overhyped and overrated 'supergroups' of the past would've given their best press clippings to record."

The album reached #3 in US and sold over three million copies. Three singles were released. Both "Handle With Care" and "End of the Line" reached #2 in *Billboard*'s Mainstream Rock Tracks chart; "Heading for the Light" reached #7 in the same chart.

In between the release of the two Wilburys' albums, a nonalbum track, "Nobody's Child," appeared on *Nobody's Child: Romanian Angel Appeal*, a charity compilation raising funds for the Romanian Angel Appeal Foundation, an organization founded by Harrison's wife, Olivia, to help with the plight of Romanian orphans. The song, a country weeper about a blind orphan, was first recorded by Hank Snow in 1949; the Wilburys' version is plaintive without being mawkish.

Traveling Wilburys Vol. 3 is a rawer outing than the band's first album. "The Wilburys may sound relaxed, but they don't trust anyone," Jon Pareles wrote in the *New York Times*, though the rough-and-tumble atmosphere does include a message song about the decaying environment ("Inside Out") as well as a goofy dance number, "Wilbury Twist." The album did a little less well than its predecessor, reaching #11 in the US and selling one million copies. Of the singles, "She's My Baby" fared the best, peaking at #2 in *Billboard*'s Mainstream Rock Tracks chart (it also featured the nonalbum track "Runaway" as a B-side); "Inside

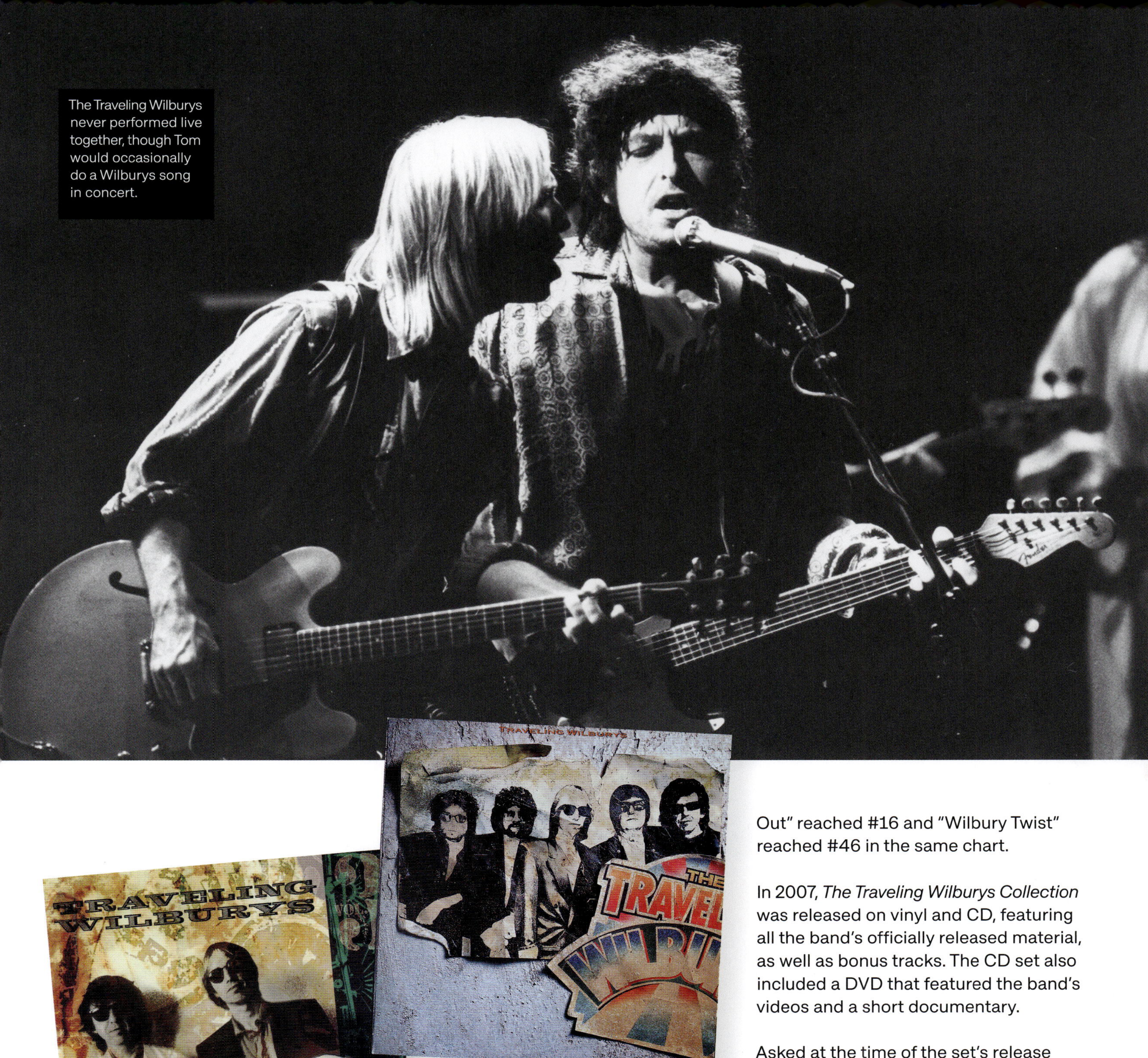

The Traveling Wilburys never performed live together, though Tom would occasionally do a Wilburys song in concert.

Out" reached #16 and "Wilbury Twist" reached #46 in the same chart.

In 2007, *The Traveling Wilburys Collection* was released on vinyl and CD, featuring all the band's officially released material, as well as bonus tracks. The CD set also included a DVD that featured the band's videos and a short documentary.

Asked at the time of the set's release about being in the Wilburys, Tom said, "Well, it probably seems like things that were that special just don't go on and on. I'm just glad that the work that we did holds up. It still warms my heart to hear it and I think it makes a lot of people happy and that's the nicest part of it."

34

Tom was photographed for the UK music paper *NME* in New York City in May 1989.

"I DIG THIS RECORD SO MUCH"

FULL MOON FEVER

APRIL 24, 1989

Tom couldn't believe it. He'd finished his debut solo album, a record he felt featured some of his best work, and his record label had rejected it. There weren't any potential singles, the label execs told him. Nothing like that had ever happened to Petty before.

Tom hadn't been planning to make a solo album. But when Jeff Lynne was in LA in late 1987, the two began hanging out and eventually starting working on songs together. One day, Tom played Jeff "Yer So Bad," a song he'd been working on, which Jeff quickly helped him finish. The next day, "Free Fallin'" came together. They decided to record the songs at Mike Campbell's home studio, bringing him into the project. As it was the holiday season, Tom didn't want to take the time to track down the rest of the Heartbreakers, instead tapping Phil Jones, the band's touring percussionist, to come in and play drums.

In contrast to making records with the Heartbreakers, recording *Full Moon Fever* was far more relaxed. "It was just a real pleasure to make this record," Tom told the *Gainesville Sun*. "There was never a day that was tense, or pressured, or anything. It was just kinda 'us out in the garage having fun.'" Petty and Lynne proved to be great collaborators, writing most of the album's songs together. "They kept writing them and we kept recording them," Jones recalled. At one point, while "Free Fallin'" was being mixed, the two were so anxious to get going on their next song that they went into an adjoining room to write "I Won't Back Down."

When Tom decided that he didn't want to recut the songs with the other Heartbreakers, "I just called them up and said, 'I'm making a solo record.'" There were some hard feelings, but Howie Epstein ended up providing backing vocals on two tracks, and Benmont

Tench played piano on "The Apartment Song." George Harrison and Roy Orbison also made guest appearances. Working with Jeff Lynne gave the record a lighter touch, the layered guitars and vocal harmonies bringing an additional sheen, from the laid-back sarcasm of "Yer So Bad" to the Bo Diddley–esque beat of "A Mind with a Heart of Its Own," to the bright punch of the turbo-charged "Runnin' Down a Dream."

The album, initially called *Songs from the Garage*, was planned for release in 1988. But then the Traveling Wilburys project took off. And there were those

On stage at the Kingswood Music Theatre in Maple, Ontario, September 1989.

pesky label executives who didn't like the record. But a happy ending was waiting in the wings. Irving Azoff stepped down as MCA's chairman, replaced by Al Teller, and the new regime gave a thumb's up to Petty's work, though they asked that he record some more songs for the album. Tom readily agreed. One of the new tracks recorded was a cover of the Byrds' "Feel a Whole Lot Better," which was so faithful to the original that the band's Roger McGuinn thought it was the Byrds' own rendition.

Full Moon Fever reached #3 on its release, selling over five million copies in the US, Tom's second-highest selling album after *Greatest Hits*. Four of the album's singles reached the Top 10 in *Billboard*'s Mainstream Rock Tracks chart, while "I Won't Back Down," "Runnin' Down a Dream," and "Free Fallin'" all reached the Top 30 in the magazine's Hot 100 chart. It was sweet vindication after being told the album had no discernable hits. As an in-joke, there was a brief spoken word segment on the CD version between tracks five and six, with Petty stating that this was the point where the album would be turned over, if you were playing the LP or cassette version.

Making the album had been a nice break for Tom, but he made it clear his band was still a going concern. "I'm still very much in the Heartbreakers," he told *Rolling Stone*. "I wouldn't think of performing with another group."

Mike and Tom get down to business with their matching Gibson Firebirds during the 1989 "Strange Behavior" tour stop in Irvine, California.

REBELS WITHOUT A CLUE

TOURING WITH THE REPLACEMENTS

SUMMER 1989

When the Replacements signed on to open for the Heartbreakers during the summer of 1989, each act ended up getting more than they bargained for.

The Replacements were a Minneapolis-based alternative rock foursome who started out as a trio named Dogbreath in 1978; by 1980, they'd become the Replacements (nicknamed the 'Mats by their fans). After building a local, then a national following, they moved from indie Twin/Tone Records to Warner Brothers subsidiary Sire Records in 1985. Their second album for the label, 1989's *Don't Tell a Soul*, had three singles that reached the Top 30 in *Billboard*'s Modern Rock Tracks chart, with the song "I'll Be You" not only topping that chart, but the Mainstream Rock Tracks chart as well.

But the album's sales had been slow, and it was thought an opening slot on Petty's upcoming tour might provide a boost. And so the Replacements signed on for what was aptly called the Strange Behavior Tour, which kicked off on July 5 in Miami. The tour was promoting Petty's *Full Moon Fever* album, and though a solo release, he was nonetheless touring with the Heartbreakers.

At first, things seemed to go well. On opening night, the two bands playfully bantered together; when Replacements' bassist Tommy Stinson asked Petty if he was nervous, he replied, "I'm scared as shit." Heartbreakers keyboardist Benmont Tench was a big enough fan of the Replacements that he occasionally joined them during their set, causing Stinson to crack, "It's nice to have a real musician onstage once in a while," at one show. Petty reciprocated, inviting Paul Westerberg (lead vocalist and guitarist) and Bob "Slim" Dunlap (guitarist) to jam with him onstage, and watching the Replacements playing their own set. "Tom liked having the spark of this upstart new band on the road," said Dunlap.

But it didn't take long for tensions to surface. The Replacements felt disoriented playing the large arenas the Heartbreakers could fill. They were also nonplussed by the typical hazard of opening for a more commercially successful band; most

Tom with Paul Westerberg, left, and Tommy Stinson, right, of the Replacements. When the two bands toured together, each got more than they bargained for.

of the audience doesn't arrive until the headliner hits the stage. And they couldn't relate to the Heartbreakers' level of professionalism, dutifully going through a preplanned setlist with little apparent spontaneity. "It was the opposite of what we were," Westerberg told the band's biographer, Bob Mehr.

So, in true Replacements style, they decided to mix it up, playing whatever songs they wanted, however they wanted, and generally goofing off. Tench, knowing the band was capable of playing a great show, was surprised: "I didn't understand why they would just thumb their nose at the whole experience." Substance abuse issues were also becoming more of a problem for the Replacements. When Petty gave Westerberg the hat he wore in the "I Won't Back Down" video, Paul later bragged that he'd traded it for drugs.

When playing Nashville on August 5, the Replacements trooped onstage wearing the clothes of the Heartbreakers' wives, which they'd illicitly acquired. At one point during their set, Westerberg, wearing a denim skirt, announced, "Last night Tom Petty told us if we fuck up again we're fired. Well, fuck you Tom Petty—and fuck you, Nashville!" But despite the threat, the band was not fired. Nor did any of their subsequent behavior—vandalizing dressing rooms, playing sets that were either too short or too long—get them booted. Instead, they faced a worse fate: being forced to remain on the tour until the very end.

Petty may have been somewhat amused by their behavior. In reference to the Replacements' destructive tendencies, he joked he'd never paid for so much broken furniture before. And he also listened to the group more than they might have realized; the phrase "a rebel without a clue," from their song "I'll Be You" later turned up in Petty's "Into the Great Wide Open."

"ANOTHER TIMELESS PETTY CLASSIC"

"FREE FALLIN'"

OCTOBER 27, 1989

Ironically, the album that some misguided MCA execs told Tom didn't have hits on it turned out to feature his biggest commercial hit of all.

Tom had just finished working on "Yer So Bad" with Jeff Lynne. When the two got together the following day, Tom began playing around with a riff on a keyboard. Jeff suggested dropping one of the chords, and Tom next began improvising lyrics about an all-American girl, who loves her mother, Jesus, and, of course, Elvis—just trying to make Jeff smile, he later explained. When he got to the chorus, Jeff came up with the phrase "free falling" and suggested Tom go up an octave when he sang it.

"So I took my voice up an octave or two, but I couldn't get the whole word in," Tom told *Billboard*. "So I sang 'freeee,' then 'free falling.' And we both knew at that moment that I'd hit on something pretty good. It was that fast." When Jeff went home, Tom finished up the lyrics. The song was recorded the next day at Mike Campbell's home studio.

The elegiac number has the narrator casting a world-weary eye on what he sees around him: vampires, bad boys, and good girls. The setting is Los Angeles, with Petty namechecking the neighborhood of Reseda and the streets Ventura Boulevard and Mulholland Drive places where he could observe "life's great pageant" as he put it: "I tried to grab a little bit of these characters on the road and it was kind of how I saw it.. the skateboarders and the shoppers and the young kids in the trendiest possible clothes and the auto-tellers and the drive-thru banks."

Yet if it's a world of plenty—in the song's video, Tom is seen playing his guitar and singing while strolling through LA's Westside Pavilion mall—it also feels emotionally bereft. The good girls are

left alone with broken hearts, with the bad boys (including the narrator) seemingly impervious to their pain. The song's narrator vacillates between regret for leaving his girlfriend and not missing her at all; in the end, he opts for temporary oblivion, leaving the world "for a while." The moment when Tom's voice reaches up to hit the high note in the song's chorus is one of the standout vocal moments in his career. But is it a call celebrating one's newfound freedom or a cry for help? The lush, layered vocal harmonies, courtesy of Petty and Lynne, help make this bitter pill go down easier.

On its release, "Free Fallin'" became Tom's highest-charting single on *Billboard*'s main chart; it also topped the magazine's Mainstream Rock Tracks chart. It quickly became a fixture in Tom's setlists, making its live debut before it was even released as a single, when Petty and the Heartbreakers performed it on *Saturday Night Live* in May 1989 (when his label would have much preferred that he play his current single, "I Won't Back Down"). Another notable performance came at that year's MTV Video Music Awards on September 6, 1989, when Guns N' Roses singer Axl Rose and the band's guitarist Izzy Stradlin joined Tom and the band for both "Free Fallin'" and "Heartbreak Hotel." Rose lets rip vocally, to Petty's apparent bemusement. "I thought it was kind of a shaky performance," he later recalled. "We didn't get a lot of rehearsal time."

Regardless, "Free Fallin'" was on the way to becoming one of Tom's most beloved songs. As he told biographer Paul Zollo, "There's not a day that goes by that someone doesn't hum 'Free Fallin'' to me, or I don't hear it somewhere."

At No. 7, "Free Fallin'" proved Petty's highest-charting song—and his last Top 10.

Petty set "Free Fallin'" in LA, namechecking Reseda, Ventura Boulevard, and Mulholland Drive.

37

"DELIGHTFULLY HOOK-FILLED"

Tom with one of his major influences, Roger McGuinn of the Byrds. McGuinn'sinfluence rings loud and clear on *Into the Great Wide Open*. He evenprovides backing vocals on "All the Wrong Reasons."

INTO THE GREAT WIDE OPEN

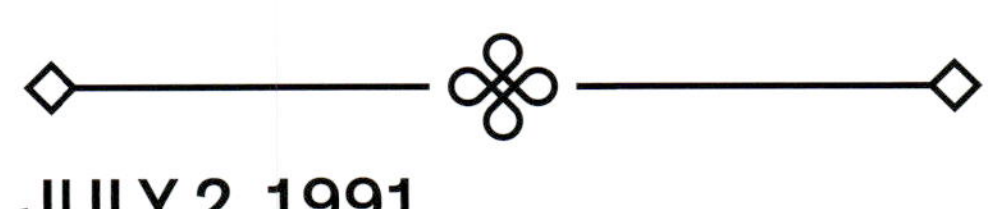

JULY 2, 1991

Jeff Lynne might have been back in the coproducer's seat. But make no mistake: the follow-up to *Full Moon Fever* was most definitely a Heartbreakers album, not a Tom Petty solo release.

Tom had no plans to leave the Heartbreakers behind. But he also felt he was, as he put it, "on a roll" working with Jeff Lynne, so the logical answer seemed to be to bring the two together. The night before the sessions began, Tom celebrated his fortieth birthday with a party, and being surrounded by his family, friends, and bandmates generated good will for the work ahead.

Everyone quickly fell into the groove of being the Heartbreakers in the studio once again. "It wasn't strange or indifferent

or anything," Tom told *CD Review*. "Just getting them to dig the trip and understand what I was doing and to trust Jeff—that was the biggest hurdle at first. But that wasn't really a hurdle. The only thing I had in the back of my mind was the hope that they'd trust me. And they did. And they were great."

Tom described the album as having a more melodic feel than *Full Moon Fever*. That was certainly evident on what would become the record's opening track (and a live favorite), "Learning to Fly," cowritten with Lynne. The song's buoyant sound was achieved by overdubbing layer after layer of acoustic guitars; close your eyes and you can even envision a plane taking off into a sunny sky. Other songs, such as "Kings Highway," maintain this bright, upbeat mood. Elsewhere, the Byrds influences are clear in the beautiful harmonies of "You and I Will Meet Again" (and an actual Byrd, Roger McGuinn, provides backing vocals on "All the Wrong Reasons"). Those wanting the band to kick it up a notch are rewarded with "Out in the Cold" and "Makin' Some Noise," lively rockers that allow the Heartbreakers to get a little frisky. The title track was a sardonic tale of the rise and fall of a would-be rock star, Eddie, clearly drawn on Petty's own experiences with the ups and downs of the music industry ("A&R man said, 'I don't hear a single'").

Into the Great Wide Open reached #13. Though receiving some good reviews (*Rolling Stone* called the album "exquisite"), others were more mixed, critics feeling that Lynne's influence resulted in songs that were deemed too formulaic. And the sales were disappointing in comparison to *Full Moon Fever*'s; *Into the Great Wide Open* had certified sales of just two million. "Learning to Fly" reached #28 and topped *Billboard*'s Mainstream Rock Tracks chart.

The album's title track only reached #92, but hit the Top 10 in the Mainstream Rock Tracks chart, peaking at #4. The single's video was an elaborate production, the band working with Julien Temple (who had also directed the video for "Learning to Fly"). Tom is cast as a rather professorial narrator, wearing round spectacles and a top hat, with Eddie, the "rebel without a clue," played by Johnny Depp. The video also featured Faye Dunaway and cameos by Matt LeBlanc, Terence Trent D'Arby, and Chynna Phillips; even Petty's real-life manager, Tony Dimitriades, makes an appearance. The song was extended to relate Eddie's story in more depth, and Tom cited it as one of his favorite videos, later telling *Rolling Stone* it was "one of the only times I've ever felt fulfilled by a video. I even had people coming to me wanting to make it into a movie."

Though not officially released as singles in the US, "Out in the Cold" and "Kings Highway" reached #1 and #4, respectively, in the Mainstream Rock Tracks chart, due to radio airplay.

Into the Great Wide Open was the first Heartbreakers album in four years. Another five years would pass before the next Heartbreakers album was released.

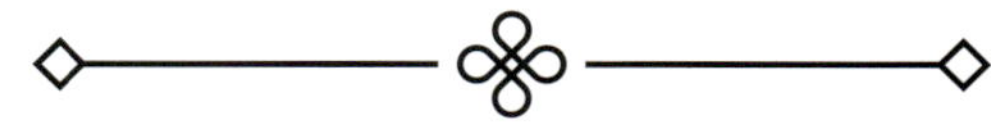

MAKING SPIRITS BRIGHT

THE CHARITY CHRISTMAS SONG

OCTOBER 20, 1992

On stage at the Kingswood Music Theatre in Maple, Ontario, September 1989.

Tom did acknowledge the influence of the classic Phil Spector–produced classic, *A Christmas Gift for You*.

When Tom was asked to record a song for a Christmas charity compilation, he didn't want to take the easy route and record a cover song or a traditional carol. He wanted to do something special. So he decided to write an original song.

In 1987, A&M Records released the first *A Very Special Christmas* album. The idea for the release came from producer Jimmy Iovine, whose wife, Vicki, suggested that the album's proceeds benefit the Special Olympics (a sports organization that runs events for people with disabilities). Contributors on the first compilation included Eurythmics, Whitney Houston, the Pretenders, and Bruce Springsteen.

The album was a success, eventually selling over four million copies. So *A Very Special Christmas 2* was planned for release in 1992. Given Iovine's previous work with Petty, it was natural for him to approach Tom for a song.

"I didn't want to do somebody else's song," Tom later explained in the liner notes for the *Playback* box set. "To me and Mike [Campbell] there's only one Christmas album in the pop field and that's Phil Spector's. . . . That really sounds like Christmas to me." He's referring to the classic 1963 album *A Christmas Gift for You from Phil Spector*, featuring recordings by such artists as the Ronettes, the Crystals, and Darlene Love, all featuring Spector's trademark "Wall of Sound" technique, repeatedly overdubbing instruments and vocals to create a lush, orchestral sound.

Tom sat down to compose "Christmas All Over Again" when he was in Florida in the summer of 1992. Unusually, he not only wrote the song on a ukulele, it was also an instrument that George Harrison had given him, after teaching him how to play it. "The ukulele is a really cool instrument, even though it doesn't have that image," Petty observed. Back in LA, Tom rehearsed the song with Heartbreakers, and Iovine, who coproduced the track, booked additional musicians for the session. There would be total of twenty-three musicians on the track. It was more than enough to create a suitable "wall of sound" feeling—especially as the recording used a number of instruments not typically found on a Heartbreakers record (harpsichord, marimba, harp, and bells).

Tom described the session as "a lot of fun," but with so many contributors, the end result was "pretty much a mess." That's when he brought in Jeff Lynne, who helped him redo the lead vocal "and tidy it up just a little bit"; Lynne also provided backing vocals and played bass, bells, and timpani on the track.

Anyone familiar with the Spector holiday album will recognize its influence from the first bars of "Christmas All Over Again"; after the opening drum roll, you half expect to hear Ronnie Spector start singing. It's a song celebrating the communal aspects of the holiday, a time when "Everybody's singin'," putting up decorations, and gathering under the mistletoe, with a few dollops of humor thrown in along the way (those relatives you've missed, but that you don't want to kiss). During the song's fade-out at the end, Tom even mentions a few things on his own Christmas list: "I want a new Rickenbacker guitar . . . two Fender Bassmans . . ."

In addition to its appearance on *A Very Special Christmas 2* (which sold over two million copies), the song has also appeared in the films *Home Alone 2*, *Jingle All the Way*, and *Four Christmases*. Petty later performed the song in the television special *A Very Special Christmas from Washington, D.C.*, which was taped at the White House on December 14, 2000 (he also gave a private performance for Vice President Al Gore before the taping). It's a song he looked back on with pride: "I've always been happy because every Christmas I do hear it on the radio and I really like it."

ALL THE BEST, PLUS TWO

GREATEST HITS

NOVEMBER 16, 1993

Tom's *Greatest Hits* album became a perennial bestseller from the moment of its release.

The 18-track collection featured songs from every Heartbreakers album except *Let Me Up (I've Had Enough)*, as well as three tracks from *Full Moon Fever*, despite its officially being a "solo" album. But as a condition of Petty's leaving MCA, the label asked that the album feature some new material, in order to fulfill the terms of his contract. Tom was already in the midst of recording his second solo album, *Wildflowers*, and he didn't want to draw on any of the songs he was working on for that record. So producer Rick Rubin suggested he bring in the Heartbreakers to work on new material, recording live in the studio. Over a dozen songs were recorded, with "Mary Jane's Last Dance" and a cover of Thunderclap Newman's "Something in the Air" making the final cut.

"Mary Jane's Last Dance" is a mid-tempo, bluesy number about an independent soul determined to keep moving on, featuring some nice harmonica work by Petty (though some have speculated that "mary jane" refers to marijuana). "Something in the Air" is a rather labored "protest" song endeavoring to capitalize on the revolutionary spirit of the late 1960s (the song was released in 1969), though instead of rallying behind a cause the song's protagonist sounds more interested in generating mayhem (collecting "arms and ammo" to "blast our way through here"). In comparison with the original, the Heartbreakers' cover features a stronger lead vocal by Petty.

It was the last time drummer Stan Lynch recorded with the Heartbreakers. Lynch admitted to author Warren Zanes he was a "total dickwad" during the sessions, taking exception to Rubin's request that he emulate the drum sound on the Rolling Stones' "Gimme Shelter" and feeling that his work was unappreciated. After two further live dates with the band in October, he was out for good.

Greatest Hits reached #5. *Entertainment Weekly* gave it an A+, saying that the record "bears eloquent testimony to the durability of Petty's tough-'n'-tender heartland pop." "Mary Jane's Last Dance," the first single, reached #14, also topping *Billboard*'s Mainstream Rock Tracks chart. It was accompanied by another

The two new tracks cut for *Greatest Hits* marked drummer Stan Lynch's last dance with the Heartbreakers.

Touting *Into the Great Wide Open* at London's Wembley Arena, March 23, 1992.

distinctive video, in which Petty plays a mortician behaving in a less than professional way with a corpse (played by Kim Basinger). "Something in the Air" reached #19 in the Mainstream Rock Tracks chart.

The album was reissued in 2008, with "Something in the Air" replaced by Petty's duet with Stevie Nicks, "Stop Draggin' My Heart Around." It was reissued again in 2010, with "Something in the Air" reinstated.

And in 2022, a Dolby Atmos mix of the album was released. The tracks were mixed by Ryan Ulyate, who had worked on Petty's albums from *The Live Anthology* (2009) on. "It was a joy listening to the tapes and discovering all the sonic elements that went into each song, and then presenting them in a new, compelling, and *immersive* way," Ulyate said in a press release. "The goal with this Atmos mix is simple: get people closer to the music they love, by putting them inside it! *Greatest Hits* has so many iconic recordings that fans have lived with and loved over the years. Several great producers and engineers contributed to these classic tracks. I did my best with the Atmos mix to give the music the respect it deserves, by going back to the multitrack tapes and making sure that every sound and nuance in the original stereo mix was accounted for."

After Petty's death, the album reentered the *Billboard* charts, peaking even higher than on its first release, reaching #2 in the Hot 100 and topping the magazine's Top Rock Albums chart. With sales of over twelve million, it's Tom Petty's biggest-selling album to date.

"I ALWAYS LIKED FILMS"

THE VIDEO VANGUARD AWARD

SEPTEMBER 8, 1994

Given his acclaimed work in the medium of video, it was no surprise Tom would eventually become a Video Vanguard winner.

It was no surprise that Tom was honored for his work in music video. After all, his videos were considered among the most innovative—"so iconic" in the words of director Peter Bogdanovich, who directed the Heartbreakers documentary *Runnin' Down a Dream*. And by the time he received his award from MTV for being a "Video Vanguard," he'd been making what he referred to as "promo films" for fifteen years.

Tom's first video was for the song "Refugee" (from *Damn the Torpedoes*), made for the same reason most acts make a video—to send out to various outlets so they wouldn't have to make live appearances on an endless number of television shows. It featured a straightforward performance, with Tom initially seen singing in an alley, then the whole band performing together in what appears to be an abandoned building. "We showed up with our guitars, the director said, 'Stand here,' and that was it," Tom recalled.

There wasn't much more thought put into the videos made for the next album, *Hard Promises*. Four videos were cranked out in two days, directed by Jim Lenahan, the former Mudcrutch member who went on to be Tom's stage and lighting director. By this time, there was a new outlet for such creations: Music Television, or MTV. "When MTV came along, they were so hungry for product that they began to play all those old films," Tom recalled to author Paul Zollo. "We just called them promo films, they weren't called videos. And we actually thought the term 'video' was weird, because they were on film."

By the time MTV arrived, Tom felt like an "old hand" at making videos. "But I never dreamed those things would be seen repeatedly," he said in the book *I Want My MTV*. Nonetheless, he regarded it as another field in which he could express his creativity. "I love film," he told the Associated Press. "It wasn't hard to make something better than everyone else. I was amazed at just how bad MTV was. Terrible videos and terrible songs, and most people made them almost all the same. I thought let's just get out of the box here and do something different."

That "difference" started with the "You Got Lucky" video in 1982. "No one had ever—even Michael Jackson—done a prelude to a video," Tom noted with pride about the video's extended opening sequence. "A bit of business before the song started and we never lip-sync or anything. We were sick of lip-syncing. But boy, did it explode. It really did change the way videos went."

"Don't Come Around Here No More" is likely Tom's best known video, but his video career has plenty of other highlights among the forty-plus videos he made: turning into a cartoon character in "Runnin' Down a Dream"; portraying a creepy morgue attendant in "Mary Jane's Last Dance"; the stylish troubadour in "You Don't Know How It Feels" (the latter two both VMA winners for Best Male Video in 1994 and 1995), to mention a few.

The honor was initially called the Video Vanguard Award, then named the Michael Jackson Video Vanguard Award in 1991. It was subsequently renamed the Lifetime Achievement Award, the Video Vanguard Award again, finally returning to being called the Michael Jackson Video Vanguard Award in 2011. To distinguish it from the other VMAs, the award isn't the usual silver "Moonman" (MTV's astronaut mascot) given out for other categories but is instead gold-plated.

Making videos was an obligation for rock stars in the 1980s. But as Brian Raftery wrote in *Wired*, it was nonetheless something Tom enjoyed doing, "using the medium to play up his love of detailed storytelling and southern-weirdo charms."

THE TRIBUTE ALBUM

YOU GOT LUCKY

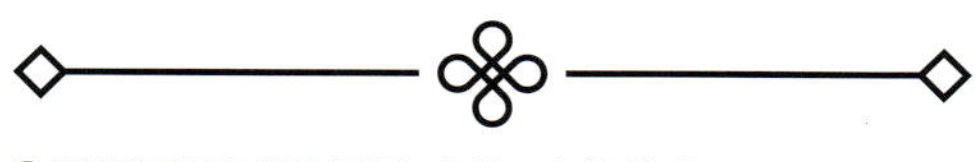

SEPTEMBER 13, 1994

You know your musical legacy is assured when you get your very own tribute album.

Seventeen years after the release of Tom's first album, *You Got Lucky: A Tribute to Tom Petty* was released on Backyard Records. It's an alternative rock take on Petty's work, with the bands digging in and transforming the songs into harder, grittier numbers. As David Browne observed in *Entertainment Weekly*, "Some of these bands take more chances on the songs than Petty does himself."

The album kicks off with a bracing version of "American Girl" by Portland act Everclear. You can imagine the song's protagonist roaring off on her motorcycle, as Art Alexakis howls, "We can last all goddamn night!" Another highlight comes from Seattle-based Silkworm, who, working with Steve Albini (Nirvana, PJ Harvey) as producer, turn the romanticism of "Insider" (Petty's duet with Stevie Nicks) into a dark and brooding recitation. And speaking of Petty/Nicks duets, Chicago's Loud Lucy take on "Stop Draggin' My Heart Around" and turn it into a crunchy grunge anthem, with Veruca Salt's Louise Post filling Nicks' shoes.

There's a mix of Petty's best-known material alongside deeper album cuts. Seattle's Engine Kid adopt the loping rhythms of "Breakdown" during the verses, then get all gnarly during the choruses. Fig Dish, from Chicago, meld "Don't Come Around Here No More" into a heavier, sludgier concoction. Conversely, Dexter Methorophan's version of "Southern Accents" adheres to Petty's arrangement fairly closely.

Punchdrunk (who started out in Milwaukee and eventually ended up in NYC) pick "Nightwatchman" to grapple with; compare their raunchy take to the clipped, new wave-influenced Heartbreakers version and you might not even recognize it as the same song. Cincinnati's Throneberry toughens up "Here Comes My Girl" in comparison to the more loping, moderate rock Heartbreakers rendition. Truck Stop Love, from Manhattan, Kansas, boost the tempo of "Listen to Her Heart," but it still has the same buoyancy as the original Heartbreakers track (and it still has the line about cocaine).

"Century City" was one of the more raucous tracks from *Damn the Torpedoes*, and

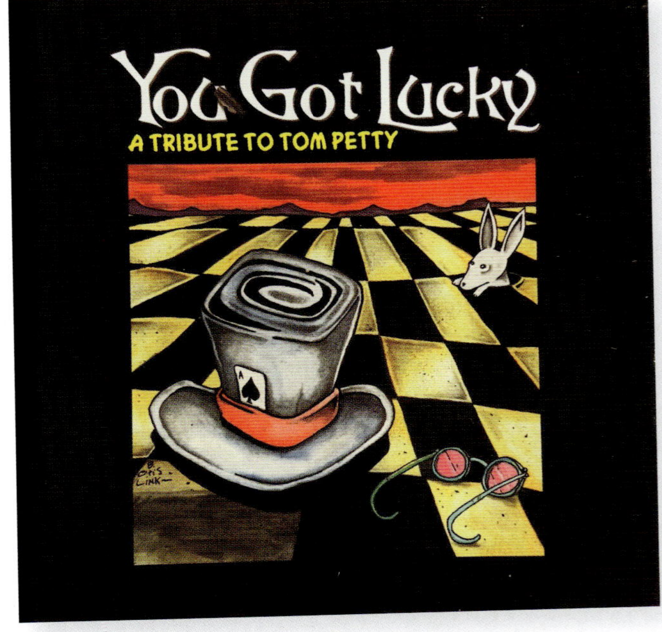

The *You Got Lucky* tribute disc featured a host of alt-rock faves. Louise Post from Veruca Salt subbed for Steve Nicks on Loud Lucy's cover of "Stop Draggin' My Heart Around"; Art Alexakis and Everclear performed the Petty classic "American Girl"; and Silkworm (Tim Midyett pictured) covered "Insider."

aMiniature, from sunny San Diego, give their version a dose of punk spirit. And Edsel, hailing from Washington, DC, get the honor of covering the title track, taking an already smoldering song and making it far more harrowing and sinister.

On its release, *You Got Lucky* attracted a range of responses. In spite of liking some tracks, David Browne also wrote that much of the album was "worth one listen and not much more." In *Round Up*, Tim Martin wrote, "*You Got Lucky* mangles almost every cool melody into a punk grinder mercilessly, making the songs sound more like a really bad rip-off of the Ramones instead of Tom Petty" (though he still liked Silkworm's "Insider" and Punchdrunk's "Nightwatchman").

Elsewhere, David Latimer's syndicated piece had nothing but praise: "But at its best, *You Got Lucky* does everything that a tribute album should—it highlights the strengths of the original while sounding new." He also singled out Silkworm's "Insider," calling it "stunning"; *Entertainment Weekly* liked it too, making the track the clear winner among the critics.

Latimer also understood the album's *raison d'être*: "seemingly playing with the idea of how Tom Petty and the Heartbreakers might sound if they were coming up today. The answer: he'd largely forsake his homegrown acoustic-electric guitar mix for some good old amplified noise."

And that's precisely what made this release a more interesting tribute album. The younger generation acts weren't trying to emulate Petty, but were more focused on finding something in the songs they could rework in their own style. It's an album designed for the indie rock crowd, not the typical Tom Petty fan. And it also illustrated how well Petty's songs could hold up in completely different musical settings.

42

‘RESOLUTE PASSION AND MATURITY”

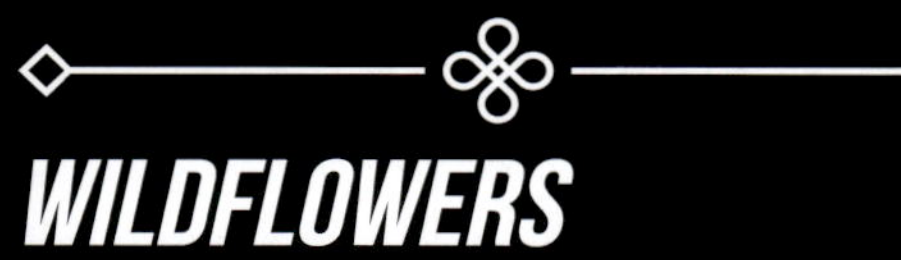

WILDFLOWERS

NOVEMBER 1, 1994

Tom’s second solo album was a record that cut ties with the past while charting a new course for the future. It was a chronicle of a decaying marriage; Tom’s daughter Adria later said that on first hearing the album, she knew her parents were about to break up. And while some of the Heartbreakers would appear on the record, there was no sign of drummer Stan Lynch. But there were beginnings as well, as Tom moved to a new record label, Warner Brothers, and took on a new producer, Rick Rubin. As Mary Wharton, director of the documentary *Tom Petty: Somewhere You Feel Free—The Making of Wildflowers* observed, “From his personal life to his business life to his creative life, Tom was trying to figure out how to put things back together in a way that made sense to him in that moment.”

Tom had been plotting to leave MCA Records since the label had initially rejected *Full Moon Fever*. On hearing Tom play “Free Fallin’” at a dinner party, Warner Brothers’ president Lenny Waronker said he’d be happy to sign him to his label. Petty agreed, and signed a secret deal with Warners that would go into effect once he had fulfilled his obligations to MCA.

Then producer Rick Rubin, who had worked with rap and heavy metal acts, got wind of the arrangement. He’d loved *Full Moon Fever* and was anxious to work with Tom. The two met, and Petty agreed it was time to take on a new coproducer. “Tom was clear he wanted it to be a solo album,” Rubin later told *Rolling Stone*. “It wasn’t clear to me why it was important to him, but he did make the point.”

He also made it clear that he did not want to work with Stan Lynch. Steve Ferrone, previously a member of the Average White Band, who later recorded and toured with Eric Clapton, Duran Duran, and George Harrison, among many others, auditioned and impressed everybody with his timing. He was in.

It was a fecund writing period for Tom. In writing the title track, he simply sat down, turned on the tape recorder, and the song came out in one go. There was no rush to complete the album, allowing Tom to “try different types of songs, more acoustic here and there, more introspective,” as Mike Campbell put it. The acoustic-based title track was far from the slicker sound of the Lynne recordings, while “You Don’t Know How

The "Dogs with Wings" tour stopped at Uniondale, New York, in April 1995, the year after *Wildflowers* was released.

It Feels" and "To Find a Friend" (the latter featuring Ringo Starr on drums) tapped into Petty's underlying despondency, balanced by numbers like the foot-stomping "Honey Bee" and the wry hopefulness of "It's Good to Be King."

Tom recorded enough material for two albums, but Waronker persuaded him to keep the record to a single album. That likely helped sales; *Wildflowers* quickly became one of Tom's best-selling albums, with over three million in sales and reaching #8. "You Don't Know How It Feels" became another of his best-loved songs, reaching #13, and topping the Mainstream Rock Tracks chart. Subsequent singles also fared well in the Mainstream Rock Tracks chart, "You Wreck Me" reaching #2, "It's Good to Be King" reaching #6, and "A Higher Place" reaching #12.

In 2012, Tom spoke to *Rolling Stone* about releasing an expanded version of *Wildflowers*. The project was finally realized in 2020 with *Wildflowers & All the Rest*, available in two-, four-, and five-disc versions. In addition to the songs that had been cut from the proposed double album, there were home recordings, alternate takes, and live versions. It offered a bounty of material for fans who wanted to explore how the album had come together.

Tom himself recognized that the album was extra special. As Benmont Tench told journalist David Browne: "He would always say, 'That's the best album we ever made.'"

FROM THE VAULTS

PLAYBACK

NOVEMBER 20, 1995

London, 1985. The tracks on *Playback* went all the way back to 1973, serving up a nice bunch of rarities for Petty fans.

Playback was a treasure trove for Tom Petty fans. The six-CD (or cassette) set spanned twenty years, including the days of Mudcrutch, songs by the Heartbreakers, and Petty's solo material. Best of all, there were plenty of rarities—non-album B-sides, tracks that were long out of print, and two CDs worth of previously unreleased material.

Greatest Hits had come out just two years before and offered a great "highlights" look at Petty's career. But *Playback* was meant to be a deep dive. It also gave MCA, who released the set, another bite of the Tom Petty apple, as Tom had moved to Warner Brothers by this point.

The first three discs were like an expanded greatest hits collection. The first CD, entitled *The Big Jangle*, covered the years 1976 to 1981; *Spoiled & Mistreated* covered 1982 to 1987; and *Good Booty* covered 1989 to 1993. It's here you'll find the expected tracks: "Breakdown," "Refugee," "Don't Come Around Here No More," "I Won't Back Down," "Free Fallin'." And you could even do a Petty compilation without including "American Girl"?

It's on the fourth disc that things start to get interesting for diehard Petty fans. Simply entitled *The Other Sides*, the disc features fifteen flip sides from Petty's singles that never appeared on an album. B-sides are sometimes dismissed as throwaways. But you couldn't say that about the yearning "Trailer," a song cut from the *Southern Accents* even though it seems a perfect fit for that album. A live version of "King's Highway" (originally from *Into the Great Wide Open*) places the number in a new acoustic setting (Mike Campbell's mandolin is a highlight), transforming it into a completely different song. A rollicking live version of "Psychotic Reaction" from 1991 is notable because it features drummer Stan Lynch on vocals.

The final two discs, *Through the Cracks* and *Nobody's Children*, feature previously unreleased material. The earliest track, "On the Street," takes you all the way back to Benmont Tench's parents' living room in Florida in 1973, when Mudcrutch recorded a demo (on a two-track reel-to-reel deck) in the hopes of attracting the attention of a record label in LA. It's a spirited number that you wish the Heartbreakers had recorded a studio version of (a live version does appear on *Live at the Fillmore 1997*).

It was the first official release of material by Mudcrutch since the "Depot Street" single. You also get to hear the band's version of "Don't Do Me Like That," a clear blueprint of the Heartbreakers' later version; indeed, some might argue that this early rendition is more powerful. And speaking of early versions, you can hear how "Stop Draggin' My Heart Around" would've fared as a solo track instead of a Petty/Nicks duet—quite nicely, as it turns out, the demo having more of a rock feel. "Waiting for Tonight," with superb backing vocals from the Bangles, was yet another number dropped from a Petty album (*Full Moon Fever* in this case) that deserved to make the final cut. It's no surprise to find some Elvis songs (recorded during the *Greatest Hits*) sessions, though "Wooden Heart" from *G.I. Blues* (not one of the King's better cinematic exploits) is certainly an unexpected choice. And that's just the tip of the rarities iceberg.

A VHS (later DVD) of the same name was also released, featuring seventeen of Petty's videos. Due to its wealth of unreleased material, *Playback* has remained a favorite release of Petty fans. Though now out of print, at the time of writing it could be found at various online resellers, at prices starting from $40. In comparison to other artists' anthology-styled releases, *Playback* was a set that earned special praise for its lack of filler. As *Ultimate Classic Rock* wrote, "But where many retrospective boxes have always tended to lard their later discs with less compelling material, this one offered every indication that Petty remained at peak power, and poised for another run of classic records."

TAKING HOME THE HONORS

THE GRAMMY WIN

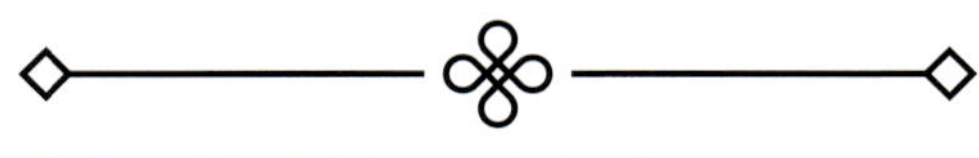

FEBRUARY 28, 1996

"You Don't Know How It Feels" was Tom's last Top 40 hit. It was also the song that gave him his first solo Grammy.

Tom's first Grammy nomination came in 1982, when "Stop Draggin' My Heart Around" was nominated for Best Rock Performance by a Duo or Group with Vocal. In 1990, *Full Moon Fever* and "Free Fallin'" were nominated for, respectively, Album of the Year and Best Rock Vocal Performance, Male. He first captured a Grammy when *Traveling Wilburys Vol. 1* won Best Rock Vocal Performance by a Duo or Group, but that was jointly shared with his fellow Wilburys (the record was also nominated for Album of the Year, but lost to Bonnie Raitt's *Nick of Time*). More nominations followed, for his own "Learning to Fly" (Best Rock Song), "Into the Great Wide Open" (Best Rock Vocal Performance by a Duo or Group), and another nomination for his participation in an all-star performance of "My Back Pages" at a Bob Dylan tribute concert on October 16, 1992, celebrating the thirtieth anniversary of Dylan's self-titled debut album.

So it must have been enormously satisfying to finally receive his own award. Ironically, Petty later said he almost left the song off the album. It's the kind of reflective number that conjures up visions of a late night drive with a friend, not least because of the reference to going on a "moonlight ride." It's a breakup song that's less about the dissolution of a relationship than it is about the need to have someone to connect with afterward—a person who might not know how it feels but is going to be there for you regardless. It's a song about camaraderie.

The song was the first single released from *Wildflowers* (which was also nominated for a Grammy for Best Rock Album; it lost out to Alanis Morissette's *Jagged Little Pill*). It was thought the line "roll another joint" might impede radio play, so a version with the line changed to "hit another joint" was distributed to radio stations. But the line wasn't changed in the song's video, so MTV did its own edit, reversing the word "joint" in the playback, to Tom's surprise.

Tom preparing for that evening's show at the Target Center in Minneapolis on September 10, 1995.

"I wrote this song not thinking that it was controversial in any way," he said when he appeared on *VH1 Storytellers*.

It's an up-close-and-personal video, with a tight close-up of Tom singing directly to the camera (in between playing the occasional mournful line on the harmonica). Throughout the song, there's a changing panorama behind him, initially a blurred background that gradually comes into focus, revealing a variety of activities going on: couples kissing, a man watering oversized flowers, even a bank robbery. At one point, Petty's even shoved aside in his own video, as a scantily clad young woman (actress Raven Snow), takes command of the mic to lip-sync a few lines. And despite their censorship, the clip later won MTV Video Music Award for Best Male Video.

"You Don't Know How It Feels" reached #13 in *Billboard*'s Hot 100 and topped the magazine's Mainstream Rock Tracks chart. Tom would receive another eight Grammy nominations, but there would be only one further win, when the film *Runnin' Down a Dream* won Best Music Video, Long Form, in 2009. A home recording of "You Don't Know How It Feels," discovered in Petty's archives, was released in 2020; it reached #54 on the iTunes chart.

45

"I FOUND AN ANGEL"

THE GEORGE AND IRA GERSHWIN AWARD CEREMONY

APRIL 26, 1996

On stage at the Target Center, Minneapolis, Minnesota, September 10, 1995.

Of the various awards Tom Petty received throughout the course of his career, receiving the George and Ira Gershwin Award for Lifetime Musical Achievement was one of the most prestigious—and unusual.

Together and separately, the Gershwin brothers were responsible for writing an impressive number of songs and other musical works now considered standards: "I Got Rhythm," "They Can't Take That Away from Me," "Someone to Watch Over Me," the opera *Porgy and Bess*, the orchestral piece "An American in Paris."

In 1988, the University of California, Los Angeles, founded the George and Ira Gershwin Award in recognition of their musical accomplishments and as a thank you for writing the university's fight song (the Gershwins' song "Strike Up the Band" was rewritten as "Strike Up the Band for UCLA" in 1936). The award is meant to honor "living musical artists whose contributions in the field of popular song exemplify the standard of excellence associated with George and Ira Gershwin" (and it's not to be confused with Library of Congress Gershwin Prize for Popular Song).

Broadway, television, and film star Angela Lansbury was the award's first recipient. Other recipients include Ella Fitzgerald, Ray Charles, Julie Andrews, and Frank Sinatra. But Tom set a new standard by being the first rock artist to receive the award, thus opening the door for later recipients Brian Wilson and the Who's Pete Townshend and Roger Daltrey.

The award ceremony was held at UCLA on April 26, 1996. Tom, soberly attired in black and wearing glasses, came onstage to an enthusiastic reception. He spoke of his love of music: "It's a truly magical thing and all these years I've done it, it's only recently that I really understand the power and the magic and the beauty of the music." He then shared an anecdote about working on Johnny Cash's *Unchained* album, when Carl Perkins dropped by. Perkins spoke of being in heaven with his fellow musicians one day, adding, "When you get there Tom, I'm gonna give you the best guitar God's got," a sentiment Petty found touching.

"Whatever your concept of God is, I believe that he writes the songs," Petty continued, "and it's just sent down through me, you know, and other songwriters. I feel like a receiver; and tonight I'm really grateful to receive this award."

George and Ira Gershwin wrote some of the twentieth century's most notable music works, from the opera *Porgy and Bess* to "Rhapsody in Blue."

He also had a surprise. Before getting on stage, he'd asked if an electric guitar and amplifier could be provided; a student willingly obliged by rushing back to his dorm room to lend his own gear to Petty. When the right moment arrived, Tom announced, "I feel really nervous without a guitar on stage," and the guitar was brought on stage for him. "Now I feel better," he continued. "I'll play you a brand new song."

The audience was then graced with the debut performance of "Angel Dream." It's in a higher key than the recorded version that appears on the *She's the One* soundtrack, and, with only Petty's voice and a single guitar, it's a stripped-down rendition that has a haunting delicacy. Though a quiet and introspective song, a few people can't resist calling out the occasional "Woo!" At the song's end, Petty calls out "God bless ya!" and makes his exit.

Tom had acknowledged in his speech that while he didn't own any of George and Ira Gershwin's own recordings, "I do appreciate their work." But it would be a surprise if he didn't have at least some of their music in his record collection—perhaps *Cheap Thrills*, by Big Brother and the Holding Company, which features Janis Joplin's exquisite version of "Summertime," or one of the many recordings of George's majestic "Rhapsody in Blue." In winning an award named after such composers, Petty truly was in stellar company.

"A REALLY KIND OF CONFUSED ALBUM"

AUGUST 6, 1996

Tom's soundtrack for *She's the One* was probably the most curious outing of his musical career. Even he seemed uncertain about how he ended up making the record. Asked by Paul Zollo why he decided to take the project on, he replied, "I often wonder."

The ball began rolling when Tom was approached to work on a soundtrack for director Ed Burns' new romantic comedy *She's the One*. Tom had enjoyed Burns' previous work, the film *The Brothers McMullen* in particular, and found *She's the One* to be "a really charming little film." He agreed to serve as the film's musical director.

That turned out to be a bit more than he could handle. In addition to his own work, Tom was expected to reach out to other artists and get them to contribute songs to the score. Tom disliked having to make these kind of calls, and considered dropping out of the project. But producer Jimmy Iovine convinced him that he'd be able to do it all himself, telling Petty, "You should do it, but like Paul Simon did for *The Graduate*. Hey, bang it out. It'll be easy."

That didn't exactly prove to be true. Tom was now working to a deadline and felt rushed. "I was completely off my game," he admitted to Warren Zanes. He drew on material that hadn't made the final cut of *Wildflowers* and brought the Heartbreakers in to provide overdubs and work on some new songs. The band hadn't yet found a permanent replacement for Stan Lynch, so there ended up being four drummers on the album: Lynch, Curt Bisquera, Steve Ferrone (who'd soon be tapped to join the Heartbreakers full-time), and Ringo Starr on "Hung Up and Overdue" (which further benefits from having the Beach Boys' Carl Wilson on harmony vocals).

And unusually for a Heartbreakers record, there were also a few covers, a nicely brash take on Lucinda Williams' breakup song "Change the Locks" and an appropriately mournful version of Beck's puckishly-titled "Asshole."

Tom met his deadline. But to his disappointment, though the film's release was pushed back, it was decided to issue the record right away, even though the album would be promoting a film no one could see yet. As a result of the marketing confusion (Tom noted the album was placed only in the "soundtrack" section of stores, where most of his fans wouldn't expect to find a Heartbreakers record), sales were down. The record peaked at #15, Tom's lowest charting album since 1987's *Let Me Up (I've Had Enough)*. The singles fared better on the Mainstream Rock Tracks chart, with both "Walls (Circus)" and "Climb That Hill" reaching #6; "Change the Locks" reached #20 in the same chart.

When the album was reissued in 2021 in honor of its twenty-fifth anniversary, it was completely reworked. Instead of the original's fifteen songs, the new version cut seven songs from the original album, primarily the songs that had come from

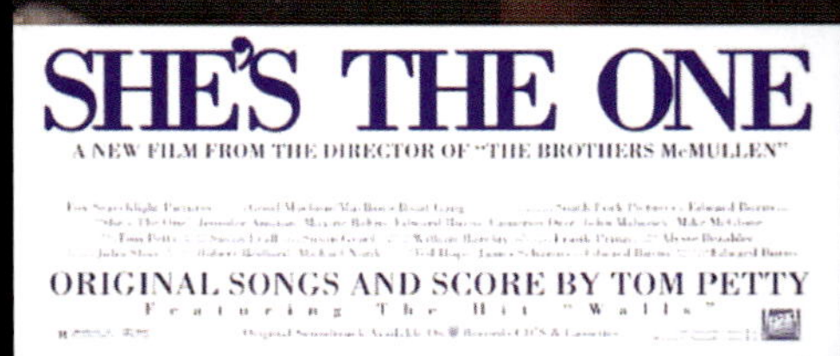

A southern boy down South: Tom at the Lakewood Amphitheater in Atlanta, Georgia, April 15, 1995.

the *Wildflowers* sessions, as they now appeared on the *Wildflowers and All the Rest* release. They were replaced by four previously unreleased tracks: outtakes of "105 Degrees" and "One of Life's Little Mysteries," the instrumental "French Disconnection," and a dive into the blues via a cover of J.J. Cale's "Thirteen Days." The album was also given a new title, *Angel Dream*, as well as a new cover.

Ryan Ulyate, who coproduced *Angel Dream*, conceded that *She's the One* "kind of left a bad taste in [Tom's] mouth, and he wished he could have gone back and really done it properly." Speaking of *Angel Dream*, Ulyate added, "I personally just feel he'd be happy with the way this came out."

47

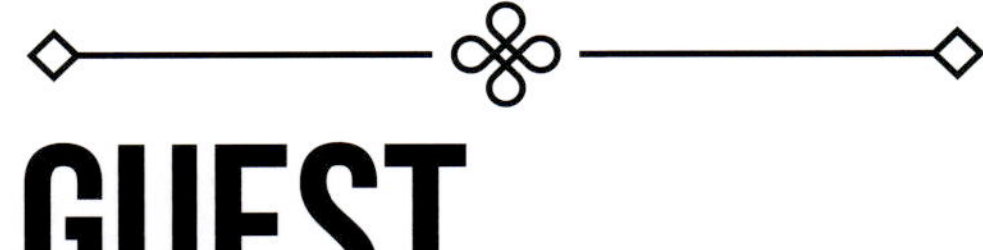

GUEST STARRING

JOHNNY CASH'S *AMERICAN II: UNCHAINED*

NOVEMBER 2, 1996

Tom in the studio with Johnny Cash, right, and *American Recordings* producer Rick Rubin.

Johnny Cash's career was revived in the 1990s when he signed with Rick Rubin's label American Recordings and released a series of albums that found success on both the country and pop charts. And Tom Petty and the Heartbreakers gave him some help along the way.

The first album in the series, *American Recordings* (1994), was a hit on the country charts and won a Grammy for Best Contemporary Folk Album. It was a solo recording—just Cash and his guitar. Cash and Rubin (who had produced the album) decided to use a band on the next record, and when Tom heard about the project, he was quick to offer his services. Eventually the rest of the Heartbreakers signed on as well.

Tom, who'd first met Cash in the early '80s, had long admired his work and was excited to get the chance to work with him. There were other connections to the Heartbreakers as well. Howie Epstein had dated Cash's stepdaughter, Carlene Carter; he and Benmont Tench had cowritten "I Fell in Love" for her. The Heartbreakers were working on the *She's the One* soundtrack at the time (which Rubin was coproducing), and the Cash sessions provided a nice break.

"Oh man, we had a ball," Tom told journalist Bill Crandall about recording *Unchained*. "What was so good was we could wander to any instrument we wanted, and did. I played the bass a lot. I played the keyboards, organ—what do they call that thing?—the mellotron." Tom didn't just play instruments; he also provided a harmony vocal on many tracks. The album was primarily made up of covers, some by country artists, such as Roy Clark's "I Never Picked Cotton," but there were also some modern numbers, such as Soundgarden's "Rusty Cage" and Petty's own "Southern Accents." "I couldn't believe he wanted to do that song," Tom said. "It made me really nervous." But all turned out well; he called the final result "beautiful. It was really full-circle for that song."

Some other musicians made guest appearances alongside the Heartbreakers, including the bassist Flea from Red Hot Chili Peppers, Lindsey Buckingham and

Mick Fleetwood from Fleetwood Mac, and country star Marty Stuart. On its release, the album reached #26 in *Billboard*'s Top Country Albums chart and went on to win a Grammy for Best Country Album.

Tom made a number of other guest appearances on records over the years, "completely by chance," as he described it. He produced Del Shannon's 1981 album *Drop Down and Get Me* and also appears on it, along with the Heartbreakers. Petty and the band also appeared on Shannon's posthumously released *Rock On!* (1991); Petty cowrote "Walk Away" for the album with Shannon and Jeff Lynne. Petty was one of four singers joining Hank Williams Jr.'s recording of his father's song "Mind Your Own Business," a #1 country hit in 1987. Petty also put in an appearance on Joni Mitchell's "Dancin' Clown," from *Chalk Mark in a Rain Storm* (1988), and harmonizes with John Prine on the title track of *Picture Show* (1991).

Petty was a huge Byrds fan and relished the opportunity to co-write "King of the Hill" with Roger McGuinn and perform on the track as well, included on McGuinn's *Back from Rio* (1991). You'll find Petty and the Heartbreakers backing Carl Perkins on *Go Cat Go!* (1996), performing on "One More Shot" and "Restless." Petty also sings on "Give Me Back My Job." He appeared on the tribute album *The Breeze: An Appreciation of J.J. Cale* (2014), with Eric Clapton on both "Rock and Roll Records" and "I Got the Same Old Blues," and singing "The Old Man and Me" on his own.

The Heartbreakers' collaboration with Johnny Cash worked out well for both sides. As Cash put it in a postcard he sent to Petty, "Tom, you're a good man to ride the river with."

Tom understandably was thrilled to get the chance to work with Johnny Cash, one of his longtime idols.

Mike Campbell and Petty at Sound City Studios for the recording of Johnny Cash's *Unchained* album.

PART 4

WON'T BACK DOWN 1997–2010

Getting down to business in Portsmouth, Virginia, on August 10, 2003.

"THE BAND WAS ON FIRE"

The opening night of the Heartbreakers' residency at San Francisco's Fillmore, January 10, 1997.

THE FILLMORE RESIDENCY

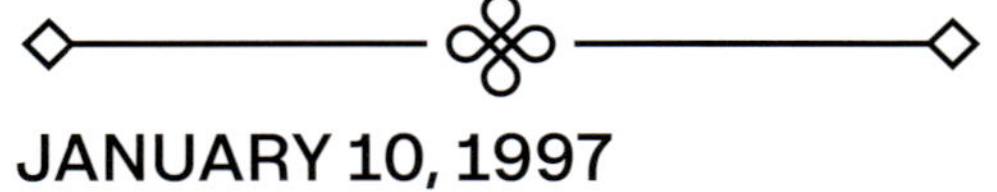

JANUARY 10, 1997

The venue the Heartbreakers played more than any other was the legendary Fillmore, where the band played a twenty-show residency in early 1997, followed by another short stand in 1999.

The Fillmore Auditorium had become a rock venue in the 1960s, under the auspices of legendary promoter Bill Graham. Led Zeppelin, the Doors, Jimi Hendrix, and Janis Joplin were just a few of many luminaries who had appeared there. The Heartbreakers' initial ten-date booking quickly expanded due to demand; the entire 1997 run was a sellout.

Tom made it clear to *San Francisco Chronicle* journalist Joel Selvin that he regarded the shows as a means to reconnect with a live audience: "I just want to play and get away from the land of videos and records for a while." This would not be a standard arena gig, with a predetermined setlist locked into place and the obligation to play the band's biggest hits. "We will play lots of covers," Petty told Selvin. "It'll be more like our soundchecks, where we play what we like." So while there would be some classics like "Free Fallin'" and "Mary Jane's Last Dance," you were just as likely to get a blast of old time rock 'n' roll like Little Richard's "Rip It Up," the garage rock of "Louie Louie," a nod to the British Invasion on "You Really Got Me," and, of course, a bit of Elvis on "Treat Me Nice." Each show became a free-form party, where no one—including the band—knew what might be played next. Which added to the fun.

Special guests livened up the proceedings as well. John Lee Hooker came over from his club across the street, the Boom Boom Room, to join the band in unfurling a bit of Mississippi Delta blues on his own "Boogie Chillen." Opening acts were brought back onstage to join the Heartbreakers during their own set. Carl Perkins was happy to join the band as they tackled his Sun Records hits, such as "Blue Suede Shoes." The Byrds' Roger McGuinn dropped in to harmonize on "It Won't Be Wrong" and "Eight Miles High."

One benefit of doing a residency is the minimal travel involved. The Heartbreakers were put up at the Miyako Hotel just two blocks away. Rehearsals were relaxed affairs that prompted new creativity. When Mike Campbell unveiled a riff he'd been working on, it quickly evolved into the song "The Date I Had with That Ugly Homecoming Queen." A sense of camaraderie developed between band and crew. Following Petty's jokey reference to being part of the "Fillmore House Band," the venue's staff quickly had hats made up bearing the phrase.

There was the occasional bump along the way. On the second night, someone set off a canister of pepper spray, and the room was cleared. But after forty-five minutes, the show went on, concluding with a raging version of "Gloria" (a fixture in the setlist from then on); Tom later referred to it as "maybe one of my best nights—ever." But for the most part, everyone was swept up in the excitement of watching one of their favorite bands having the time of their lives. The audience made their contributions too. During the February 4 show, a reveler shouted out a call for "The Heartbreakers Beach Party." The band had never even played the long-forgotten B-side live before, but the fan got his wish.

Arrangements were made to tape the final six shows. The last night was a three-hour, forty-song marathon, which was also broadcast live on radio. The 2022 album *Live at the Fillmore 1997* documented the show. A second seven-show residency was held in March 1999; footage can be seen in the home video *High Grass Dogs—Live at the Fillmore*.

It was an experience Tom would never forget. "Everybody should do this," he said after the 1997 residency. "It's going to be tough to go back to the arenas."

Tom and the Heartbreakers loved the intimacy of smaller venues like the Fillmore.

"YOU START LOSING YOUR SOUL"

GETTING CLEAN

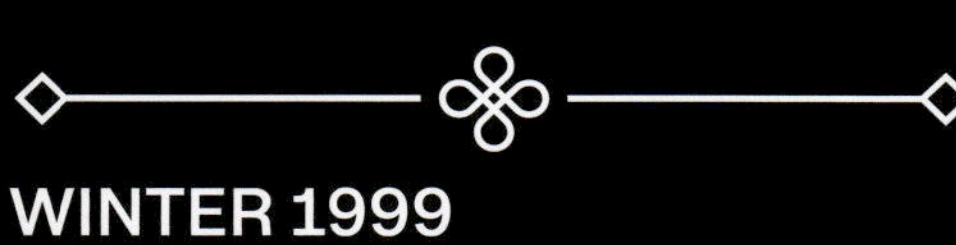

WINTER 1999

The use of illicit substances is so intrinsic to the rock world there's even a well-worn phrase about what are supposedly the key elements of rock life: "sex, drugs, and rock 'n' roll." But in the 1990s, Tom realized his drug use had become more than he could handle.

Tom's marriage to his first wife Jane officially ended in 1996. By then he'd moved out of the family home and into a smaller house in the Pacific Palisades. Petty called it the "chicken shack," a rustic cabin set on a plot of land with redwood trees and chickens wandering about. "In some places, you could actually see the daylight coming through the walls of the cabin," he told *Rolling Stone*.

"I had a lot of free time in that period," he added. Live dates had been put on hold; there was a single *Saturday Night Live* performance in 1996, the Fillmore residency in 1997, and no live dates at all in 1998. Tom worked on the *She's the One* soundtrack and the album *Echo*, but that still left him with a lot of free time. "I saw him once during that period and he seemed lost and really sad," Petty's biographer Paul Zollo said in an interview with CBC radio. What his friends didn't realize at first was that Tom's unhappiness wasn't simply due to the end of a turbulent marriage. His depression had spiraled into serious drug use.

He was certainly no stranger to drugs by that point. There was no stigma among musicians about indulging in alcohol, cocaine, LSD, and marijuana; indeed, in some cases these substances were seen as enhancing the creative process. But Tom's drug use was simply about blotting out the pain. And the drug he chose for that purpose was heroin.

People who knew him were shocked. Stevie Nicks couldn't believe it, telling biographer Warren Zanes, "I would never imagine, not in a million years, that Tom Petty would start using heroin." Producer Rick Rubin was so upset about it that he ended up telling Petty's daughters about his drug use, much to Tom's displeasure. But his friends felt helpless; Rubin had hoped his actions would be a wake-up call for Petty.

Tom managed to get through the making of *Echo*, but he later conceded his drug use had been a hindrance during the sessions. There were additional tensions as he was also hiding his addiction from his new girlfriend, Dana York, whom he would later marry. But when Dana did learn of his problem, she provided the solid support he needed. As George Harrison's widow, Olivia, later observed, "I think maybe she saved him."

After trying to kick heroin on his own, Tom admitted he needed more help. He turned to his therapist for assistance and was promptly set up in a detox program, followed by months under a doctor's care. To his everlasting relief, he was finally free.

Tom rarely spoke about his heroin addiction afterward. Though he was filmed talking about it for the *Runnin' Down a Dream* documentary, he later insisted that the scenes be cut. He finally opened up about it in *Petty: The Biography*. His main concern was that his drug use not become glamorized, telling Zanes, "If anyone is going to think heroin is an option because they know my story of using heroin, I can't do this." Zanes assured him that the point of talking about his drug use was that it would be "a cautionary tale rather than a romantic tale." Also, the main point is that it's ultimately a story of redemption, of how Tom had the strength to face up to, and then overcome, a serious obstacle in his life.

And that was the lesson Tom took from the experience. "It wasn't the best period in my life," he told *Rolling Stone*. "But I am through that. I came out the good side."

Tom in Camden, New Jersey, on June 26, 1999.

50

"SOARING HOOKS, CAPTIVATING LYRICS, GREAT GUITAR PLAYING"

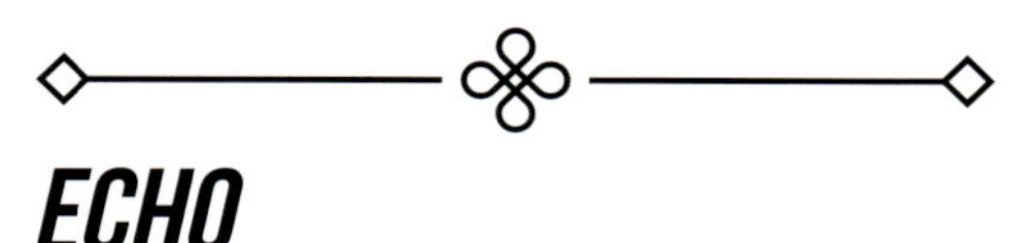

ECHO

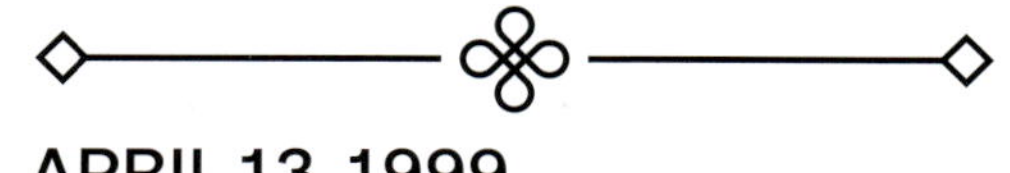

APRIL 13, 1999

Tom during his second residency at the San Francisco Fillmore, March 13, 1999, promoting the soon to be released album *Echo*.

"For the longest time, I didn't like that record," Tom said of *Echo*. "I think that my life was such a circus at that time, that I don't think I felt like I was there half of the time." The album reflected a transitional period in Tom's life, dealing with his 1996 divorce from his first wife and his new relationship with his girlfriend Dana York, whom he married in 2001. As such, *Echo* has been tagged as Tom's "divorce album," though he's pushed back against that label, telling *Rolling Stone* it was really an album about recovery.

The album was recorded at Mike Campbell's home studio, where he'd installed a Neve 1024 console. After recording a few songs there, Tom decided he liked the sound, and told Mike, "Let's keep recording here." But the sessions nonetheless proved to be a frustrating start-stop, start-stop process, with Tom writing a song, bringing it in to record, then needing to take a break to write the next song. As biographer Warren Zanes noted, the making of *Echo* "became something to get through," something made more difficult by a band leader who was admittedly only "half there." Perhaps that's why the album features a rare lead vocal by someone other than Petty; it's Mike Campbell who sings lead on the rocker "I Don't Wanna Fight."

Rick Rubin, back in the coproducer's chair, worked to provide some impromptu

The opening night of Tom's second residency at the San Francisco Fillmore, March 7, 1999.

inspiration, buying boxes of magnetic "poetry kits," where each magnet has a different word on it. The magnets were put on a metal music stand, and Tom played around with finding different phrases. One such phrase, about a "pool of sweat" and "box of pills" ended up in the moody title track.

There's a thread of melancholy that runs through the album, even on the more upbeat songs, with the opening number, "Room at the Top," setting the stage for what's to follow. "It's one of the few times I've been able to write when I was in a really bad mood," Tom told *The Album Network*. "I felt a little forlorn and I just went out in the back of my house and sat down at this little piano I have and this song rolled out." It's a song of yearning, but one not completely bereft of hope.

There's also a measure of balance provided by songs like "Free Girl Now," inspired by his girlfriend's experience of sexual harassment at work, and the freewheeling "Swingin'," which Tom

explained was completely ad-libbed, the lyric namechecking old timers Benny Goodman, Glenn Miller, and Sonny Liston.

Echo reached #10 and was certified gold. Reviews were mostly positive, with the occasional backhanded comment, as in Christopher John Farley's review in *Time*: "This CD isn't a knockout but it has punch." None of the album's singles hit *Billboard*'s main chart, but "Free Girl Now," "Room at the Top," and "Swingin'" all reached the Top 20 in the magazine's Mainstream Rock Tracks chart. "This One's for Me" and "Accused of Love" failed to chart.

It was the last record Petty worked on with Rubin. He was irritated when Rubin left the project early to work with the Red Hot Chili Peppers on their album *Californication* and so wasn't on hand to mix Petty's album. As a result, the album's production credit read: "Produced by Tom Petty and Mike Campbell with Rick Rubin." If Rick wasn't happy about it, Tom reasoned, "If you don't mix the record, you're not the producer."

It was also the last album to feature Howie Epstein. The bassist's heroin use was increasingly becoming more of a problem, to the point where he missed the cover shoot for the album and thus doesn't appear on *Echo*'s cover. The tour supporting the album would be Epstein's last with the Heartbreakers.

A STAR-STUDDED WALK

THE HOLLYWOOD WALK OF FAME DEDICATION

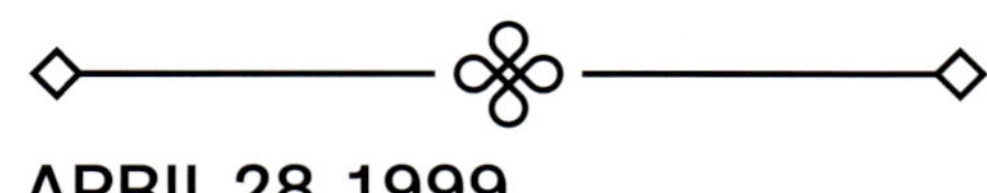

APRIL 28, 1999

Next time you're exploring Hollywood, start scanning the sidewalk when you reach the Roosevelt Hotel, at 7000 Hollywood Boulevard. That's where you'll find a star for Tom Petty and the Heartbreakers on the Hollywood Walk of Fame.

The Hollywood Walk of Fame was conceived of in 1953 by E. M. Stuart, president of the Hollywood Chamber of Commerce, who felt it would, in the words of the organization's website, help "maintain the glory of a community whose name means glamour and excitement in the four corners of the world." The walk finally became a reality on March 28, 1960, when the first star was unveiled, honoring director Stanley Kramer (*The Defiant Ones*, *Ship of Fools*, *Guess Who's Coming to Dinner*), near the intersection of Hollywood and Gower. Working out organizational details meant that the next star, for film producer Richard D. Zanuck, wasn't dedicated until December 11, 1968. But in subsequent years, dedications became far more frequent (at the time of writing, it was an average of two stars a month). The stars honor those prominent in film, television, radio, and recording.

Over the years, numerous rock legends have received stars on the Walk of Fame, including Elvis Presley, Jimi Hendrix, Queen, Janis Joplin, and the Beatles (both the group and the individual members). So Petty and the Heartbreakers would be in good company. The day of the dedication ceremony was also officially declared "Tom Petty and the Heartbreakers Day," making it a double celebration. Johnny Grant, the ceremonial "Mayor of Hollywood," hosted the event. Along with unveiling the star, Tom and band members Mike Campbell, Howie Epstein, and Benmont Tench were each given a plaque with a replica of the star.

One reason the award resonated so much with Tom was because of his strong connections to the area. The office of Shelter Records had been just down the road at 5112 Hollywood Boulevard. He'd also stayed at hotels in the area during those early days, such as the Hollywood Premiere Motel (5333 Hollywood Boulevard) and the Winona Motel (now the Hollywood Inn Express, at 5131 Hollywood Boulevard). He had strolled the streets of Hollywood a lot when he first came to California, hoping for that big break, but never knowing for sure if it would ever arrive. As he said at the ceremony, "We used to walk up and down this street and look at the stars and never dreamed we would ever have one."

Now, he did have a star. And, as he had been inspired by the stars he had seen on the Walk of Fame during those early years, perhaps some other young hopeful would be as inspired by Petty's star.

It wasn't the last time Tom was involved with a Walk of Fame ceremony. He was also on hand when stars were dedicated to George Harrison in 2009 and Jeff Lynne in 2015. After his death in 2017, Petty's star was covered with candles and floral tributes.

The Heartbreakers at their Hollywood Walk of Fame dedication.

52

“AN ANTHEM OF RESOLVE”

AMERICA: A TRIBUTE TO HEROES

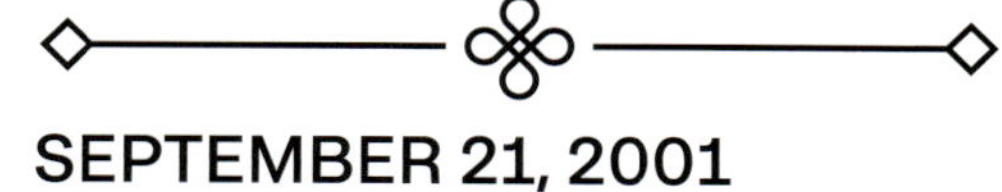

SEPTEMBER 21, 2001

It didn’t take long for musicians to respond to the tragedy of the September 11 attacks. Just ten days later, the benefit concert *America: A Tribute to Heroes* was broadcast as a telethon, raising money for the United Way’s September 11 Fund.

Actor George Clooney spearheaded the organization of the performers who would appear, including such acts as the Dixie Chicks, Stevie Wonder, Sheryl Crow, U2, Billy Joel, and Céline Dion. A range of actors also participated in the show as speakers between the performances: Sarah Jessica Parker, Chris Rock, Robert De Niro, Julia Roberts, Kelsey Grammer. The show was filmed at studios in New York, Los Angeles, and London.

Tom Petty and the Heartbreakers were the fifth act to appear. The stage was somberly set; the band performed in front of a dark backdrop, illuminated by a multitude of candles. The band members were attired in black, Tom in a white open-necked shirt. And though written over a decade earlier, the song they performed was perfect for the occasion: “I Won’t Back Down.”

As the title alone makes clear, it’s a song of resilience, of overcoming obstacles, and

Tom and the band chose to perform the fitting "I Won't Back Down" for the nationally televised *America: A Tribute to Heroes* benefit concert.

it was one of the standout tracks on *Full Moon Fever*. "That song frightened me when I wrote it," Tom told *Harp* magazine. "I didn't embrace it at all. . . . I thought it wasn't that good because it was so naked." It was so personal he wasn't sure he even wanted to record it: "But everyone around me liked the song, and it turns out everyone was right." While the initial idea came from Petty, Jeff Lynne, credited as cowriter, helped finish it up.

It turned out that while the song was drawn from Petty's own experiences, it proved to be a very universal sentiment as well. After all, everyone has faced moments of adversity in their lives, something that needed to be overcome by relying on one's own inner resources. "More people connect to that song than anything I ever wrote," Tom said in the same *Harp* interview. "I've had so many people tell me that it helped them through this or it helped them through that."

He was less pleased when then-candidate George W. Bush used the song in his 2000 presidential campaign. Petty's music publisher promptly responded with a cease-and-desist letter: "Please be advised that this use has not been approved. . . . Any use made by you or your campaign creates, either intentionally or unintentionally, the impression that you and your campaign have been endorsed by Tom Petty, which is not true." The song was subsequently dropped from the campaign.

But this was a night for unity, not division. Tom Petty and the Heartbreakers were singing for everybody across America. The number became a song of comfort—a moderate tempo rocker that talks of standing one's ground, even when facing the gates of hell, bursting into the kind of rich vocal harmonies during the chorus that tell you everything's going to be all right in the end. "'I Won't Back Down' had been an anthem for years, but performed in this capacity, it took on a far deeper meaning," wrote journalist Erica Banas. "A song already about strength and defiance hit even deeper, especially for the many brave first responders." The performance comes to a subdued ending, Tom holding his guitar up with his left hand after playing the final chord, then giving a small bow.

America: A Tribute to Heroes was broadcast on all major US networks and many cable stations, airing without commercial interruption; it would win a Peabody award as "an exceptional salute to those lost in the events of September 11, 2001." Over $200 million was raised for the United Way fund. The show was later released on CD and DVD on December 4, 2001, the album reaching #17 in *Billboard*.

"I AM TRULY HUMBLED"

At the top of the mountain: Tom on the night of his induction into the Rock & Roll Hall of Fame.

THE ROCK HALL INDUCTION

MARCH 18, 2002

"It's an honor to me because I was the kid that rock 'n' roll really meant something to," Tom told *Rolling Stone*'s David Wild about his induction into the Rock & Roll Hall of Fame. "To wind up in the Hall of Fame is just beyond all belief. I used to think—years ago, before I made records—I would be happy if I just had a good car and a place to live. It's gone *so* far past that."

It wasn't just Tom who got the honor. Past and present Heartbreakers were inducted as well: Ron Blair, Mike Campbell, Howie Epstein, Stan Lynch, and Benmont Tench. The group had been inducted in their first year of eligibility, twenty-five years after the release of their self-titled debut album, an additional honor; in contrast, fellow honoree Gene Pitney was inducted over forty years after the release of his first record. Other inductees for the "Class of 2002" included Isaac Hayes, Brenda Lee, the Ramones, Talking Heads, Chet Atkins, and Stax Records cofounder Jim Stewart.

The band gathered in Los Angeles beforehand to rehearse. It would be the first time Stan Lynch worked with the Heartbreakers since leaving in 1994, and there were understandable concerns about lingering tensions. But on his arrival at the rehearsal space, Petty greeted him with a warm hug, which helped lighten the mood, and rehearsals went well.

The ceremony was held at the Waldorf-Astoria Hotel in New York City. Tom requested Bob Dylan's son, Jakob Dylan, to make the induction speech. Jakob was hesitant about accepting, telling the band's manager, Tony Dimitriades, he didn't feel he was the right person for the job. But when Dimitriades told him he was the only person Tom had considered to make the speech, he agreed.

Tom and Heartbreakers past and present, newly inducted into the Rock & Roll Hall of Fame. From left, Benmont Tench, Mike Campbell, Petty, Howie Epstein, Stan Lynch, and Ron Blair.

During his speech, Jakob drew some laughs as he recalled sitting backstage with Petty's daughters, watching their fathers playing together, and thinking to himself, "That's gotta be so weird—Jesus, your dad is Tom Petty!" He also pointed to the band's enduring longevity. "Tom Petty and the Heartbreakers made it clear that while rock 'n' roll will have its trends, it will go through fads, it's really about the opposite; it's about being timeless . . . they truly are one of the great American rock groups."

After being introduced, each of the Heartbreakers made short statements before Tom's speech, which was also brief, running under two minutes. "I'm very proud that we're being inducted as a group, as Tom Petty and the Heartbreakers, because they're the best fuckin' band in America," he asserted, going on to thank Dimitriades for putting up with him ("I am not always a summer breeze!"), and his family. "And I thank this rock and roll for the freedom it's given me. And I thank the fans for such a wonderful life. And I thank God for all of it. God bless you, thank you very much."

The band then played a short set. Howie Epstein played bass on "Mary Jane's Last Dance"; it was the last time he'd appear with the Heartbreakers, prior to his death the following year. Ron Blair took over on bass for the band's other song, "American Girl." It was also the last time Stan Lynch would play with the Heartbreakers. He later spoke of feeling like he had "no connection" to anybody at the event. But he did send Petty a thank you letter afterward. "And it hinted at the idea that we'd be seeing more of each other," Tom told Warren Zanes. "But I never saw him or heard from him again."

Overall, it was an award Tom was pleased to receive. "It's very easy to be cynical about the Hall of Fame," he told an Associated Press reporter backstage at the ceremony. "But on the other hand, it's really a beautiful thing for someone like me. I dedicated my entire life to this music."

The Rock & Roll Hall of Fame museum opened on September 2, 1995, and has been a popular Cleveland attraction ever since.

54

"THE BAND'S MOST VIBRANT SHOWCASE IN YEARS"

THE LAST DJ

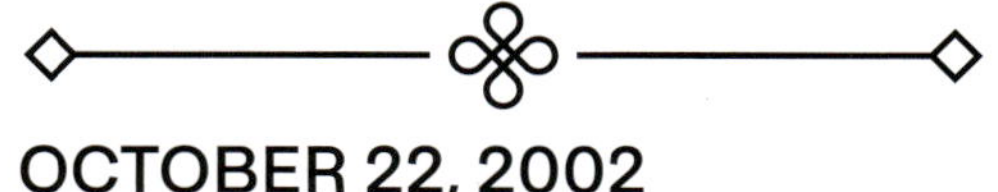

OCTOBER 22, 2002

In Atlanta, Georgia, on August 9, 2002, just prior to the release of *The Last DJ*. When some stations banned the song "The Last DJ" for being "anti-radio," Tom took it as a compliment.

Tom came out of the gate swinging on *The Last DJ*, an album that reflected his ambivalence about the world he found himself living in. "There's a huge celebration of mediocrity in our culture, and I don't remember it to this extent before," he told the *Los Angeles Times*. It was something he felt eroded personal relationships as well. "We've hit a point where I'm not sure we care about each other," he said to the *San Francisco Chronicle*'s Joel Selvin. "I miss that."

The title track presented an evocative depiction of Tom's dismay with the United States of Homogenization. The song's protagonist is an old-school disc jockey, from a time when DJs could choose for themselves what records they'd play. But there's no room for such freedom under a new regime that provides preprogrammed playlists, so the erstwhile DJ takes off and lands a job at a station in Mexico, where he can still call the shots. It's a loss not only of "freedom of choice" but also "the last human voice," Tom notes with regret.

"Money Becomes King" is another sharp-eyed critique of the music business, where the lure of the almighty dollar encourages even the purest of artists to sell out. Then there's "Joe," a taut number about a wheeling, dealing CEO always looking for next talent to exploit. But for all the apparent attacks on the music biz, the real target is greed, "this notion that we need to make all the money that is possible, of grabbing every cent. . . . It's just so unhealthy," he told the *Gainesville Sun*. He also tempered the bitterness by dropping in a few love songs, like "You and Me," saying of the album's characters, "I felt that these people had to have some hope in their lives."

Sitting in the coproducer's chair along with Petty and Mike Campbell was George Drakoulias, who got his start working with Rick Rubin and went on to produce albums by the Black Crowes, Maria McKee, and Screaming Trees. There was also a reunion with a familiar face: original Heartbreakers' bassist Ron Blair. Blair had kept in touch with Campbell over the years, and the two occasionally played and recorded together. Blair had played on Campbell's demos for "Lost Children" and "Can't Stop the Sun," so Campbell brought him to the sessions when the songs were being recorded (Petty and Campbell played bass on the other tracks). He fit right in, and Tom soon offered Ron the opportunity to rejoin the band when they went on tour to support their new album; instead of breaking in a new guy, who better to have than a former bandmate? Ron, who had come to regret leaving the band in the first place, was quick to agree.

The Last DJ reached #9, with the title track reaching #22 in *Billboard*'s Mainstream Rock Tracks chart; "Have Love Will Travel" and "You and Me" failed to chart. Even reaching the Top 30 was something of an accomplishment for "The Last DJ," as the song was banned by several radio stations owned by media conglomerate Clear Channel Communications for being "anti-radio." Which shows how thoroughly those corporate heads missed the point, for, as Petty pointed out to *Rolling Stone*, "No record has ever been made that was more pro-radio, you know." The song wasn't anti-radio; it was against what had *happened* to radio. Not that Tom was bothered by the song's being banned: "Nothing could have complimented me more."

Producer Drakoulias agreed that the album wasn't anti-anything. "You will hear some songs and you think, 'Wow, Tom's angry,'" he told *Rolling Stone*. "But, really, it's not an indictment. I think it's like, 'It doesn't have to be this way. You *can* change it.'" Meaning it was ultimately a positive album after all.

55

"GEORGE IS HERE TONIGHT"

CONCERT FOR GEORGE

Tom and his wife Dana York underneath the marquee at Royal Albert Hall for the "Concert for George" celebration of George Harrison's life. Inside, Tom shared the stage with Paul McCartney and Ringo Starr.

NOVEMBER 29, 2002

One year to the day after his death from cancer, George Harrison's friends came together in a beautiful tribute: the Concert for George.

The event was organized by Harrison's widow, Olivia, and their son, Dhani (pronounced "Danny"), who was himself a musician. Harrison's friend (and sometimes romantic rival) Eric Clapton served as the show's musical director. He put together a house band, which included himself, Jeff Lynne, and Dhani, among others. He also invited a number of special guests to participate, including Harrison's fellow Beatles, Paul McCartney and Ringo Starr, keyboardist Billy Preston—and Tom Petty and the Heartbreakers. There was no doubt Tom would be involved, as a friend of Harrison's and as a fellow

Traveling Wilbury, and the Heartbreakers were happy to come along for the ride.

London's stately Royal Albert Hall was the concert venue. Harrison's history with the hall dated back to April 18, 1963, when he played there with the Beatles; nearly thirty years later, it was the site of his last full-length concert on April 6, 1992, a benefit for the Natural Law Party. Tickets went on sale on October 11 (via telephone sales only) and promptly sold out within an hour. Proceeds benefitted Harrison's own Material World Charitable Foundation.

The evening opened with a seventy-five minute set of Indian music, reflecting one of Harrison's greatest passions. Indian musician Ravi Shankar, who gave Harrison sitar lessons, told the audience he felt Harrison's presence in the hall: "I mean, how can he not be here, when all of us who loved him so much have assembled altogether to sing for him, to play music for him? I'm sure he's here." The set featured a new number, "Arpan," that Shankar had written for the occasion. Jeff Lynne also came out during the set to provide lead vocals and guitar on Harrison's Beatle-era song "The Inner Light."

After an intermission, the show's second half opened with some comedy numbers by the Monty Python troupe. Then the house band took over, playing various Harrison numbers themselves and backing most of the special guests. Eric Clapton, serving as the emcee for the evening, welcomed the Heartbreakers to the stage, where they opened with "Taxman," from the Beatles' album *Revolver*. They followed the anti-government rant with the lovelorn "I Need You," from the Beatles' *Help!* album. Tom then brought Jeff Lynne and Dhani Harrison out to join in on the Wilburys' "Handle with Care," Petty singing Harrison's original part and Lynne singing Orbison's.

The Wilburys song drew the first big ovation of the night, though understandably the audience was most excited when Starr and McCartney came on to pay tribute to their friend, on "Photograph" (Harrison's co-write with Starr), "Something," and "All Things Must Pass." Tom and the other musicians returned to the stage for the penultimate number, "Wah-Wah," which managed to sound joyful despite its being a song of frustration, inspired by the business disagreements that engulfed the Beatles before their breakup. Everyone then remained on stage, as UK musician Joe Brown performed a gentle "I'll See You in My Dreams," accompanying himself on ukulele (an instrument that was another of Harrison's passions), as flower petals fell from the ceiling—a magical moment.

The concert was filmed and later released on CD and vinyl, and DVD and Blu-ray. "His music is known worldwide because it is just lovely music, very pure music," Tom is quoted as saying in the DVD's booklet. "Not afraid to say what's on his mind ever. I always feel lucky that I crossed paths with someone like that." In another interview, he summarized his relationship with Harrison quite simply: "He was a great guy and I miss him terribly."

"HE JUST BURNED IT UP"

PLAYING WITH PRINCE AT THE ROCK HALL

MARCH 15, 2004

Live performances are an important part of the Rock & Roll Hall of Fame induction ceremonies. And Tom got to participate in one of the event's most notable performances.

Tom was at the 2004 ceremony, held at New York's Waldorf Astoria Hotel, to posthumously induct George Harrison (sharing that duty with Jeff Lynne). Prince was also being inducted that year. Joel Gallen, the show's director and producer, thought what better song to feature in the concluding live performances than Harrison's "While My Guitar Gently Weeps"? Especially if Prince was on hand to play the song's guitar solo (which had been played by Eric Clapton in the Beatles' original recording of the song)?

Gallen wrote a personal appeal to Prince, who eventually met with him and agreed to play the song (though, ever business-minded, he asked who would have the rights to the performance. "He wanted to make sure that his performance was not exploited without his knowledge," Gallen told the *New York Times*). But during rehearsals, Gallen became concerned, when Marc Mann, a guitarist then playing in Lynne's band, stepped up to play the solo in the middle of the song and at the song's end.

After the rehearsal, Gallen approached Lynne and Petty and stressed that Mann couldn't play the solos during the show. He also spoke with Prince, who seemed unconcerned, telling Gallen, "Look, let this guy do what he does, and I'll just step in at the end. For the end solo, forget the middle solo. Don't worry about it." "And then he leaves," Gallen recalled. "They never rehearsed it, really. Never really showed us what he was going to do, and he left, basically telling me, the producer of the show, not to worry. And the rest is history."

Prince opened the show with an electrifying set that included "Let's Go Crazy," "Sign O' the Times," and "Kiss." When he concluded the performance by saying "Rock and Roll Hall of Fame, thank you so much. You've been just lovely. A real knock-out. Goodnight!," the audience might have assumed that was the last they'd see of the Purple One in action that evening. Happily, it just proved to be a warm-up. And the buildup to his appearance in "While My Guitar Gently Weeps" served to heighten the drama.

Tom took most of the lead vocal on "While My Guitar Gently Weeps" at the 2004 Rock & Roll Hall of Fame induction—then Prince stepped up and blew everyone away with his closing solo. The band hadn't rehearsed Harrison's song in its entirety, but the performance came off without a hitch.

Tom took most of the lead vocals, fronting a band that included Lynne, Mann, Harrison's son Dhani, Steve Winwood, and two of the Heartbreakers, drummer Steve Ferrone and bassist Scott Thurston, among others. Prince is unobtrusively playing off to the side. Mann performed a note-perfect rendition of the song's first solo. Then, at the three-and-a-half-minute mark, Prince comes center stage and lets fly with what Ferrone later described as "a hell of a guitar solo."

Indeed. Prince dominates the action, flashing a quick grin at Tom at one point, clearly enjoying himself. He leans back into the crowd, the audience holding him up, as the rest of the musicians "freaked out," in Ferrone's words, thinking he was falling off the stage. Then there was the moment at the song's end, when Prince threw his guitar up in the air, where it seemingly vanished. "I just saw it go up, and I was astonished that it didn't come back down again," said Ferrone. "Everybody wonders where that guitar went, and I gotta tell you, I was on the stage, and I wonder where it went, too." It later transpired that the instrument had been caught by Prince's guitar tech Takumi Suetsugu, who then handed it over to talk show host Oprah Winfrey as a gift.

Tom felt the performance had come off well; it was better that Prince take the end solo than play a note-by-note copy of the middle solo. As Gallen observed, "It became one of the most satisfying musical moments in my history of watching and producing live music."

57

"SO MUCH MORE FREEDOM"

TOM PETTY'S BURIED TREASURE

DECEMBER 2, 2004

As a devoted radio listener himself, it was no surprise that Tom ended up hosting his own show on SiriusXM Satellite Radio: *Tom Petty's Buried Treasure*.

"Hey children! Oh goodness gracious, it's Tom Petty here playing you some music" were the first words spoken by Tom on the show's debut episode, after kicking off the program playing "Bert's Apple Crumble" by Quik and "Hi-Heel Sneakers" by Tommy Tucker. "Listen, what I'm going to be doing here each week is playing you all my favorite music, just like I would do if you were over at the house, laying around, looking good. I'm going to play you everything I can think of. We're gonna go way back in time and play you some things that you might not've ever heard, some things that you might know real well. But I tell you what, it's gonna make you feel good."

Indeed, the show was like hanging out with Tom while he flipped through his extensive record collection. There were the artists you'd expect to hear: Bob Dylan ("If Not for You"), Jimi Hendrix ("Spanish Castle Magic"), and numerous songs by Elvis Presley. But he also played deeper cuts, like "True Fine Mama" by Little Richard or "Leave My Kitten Alone" by the Beatles. There was an informative element to some selections, like his playing the original version of "Hound Dog" by Big Mama Thornton, as a reminder that Presley wasn't the first to record it.

The latter aspect was something appreciated by Petty's fans. "While I enjoyed his music, it was Tom Petty the music historian who I came to respect the most," a blogger named "donkeypong" wrote, calling the show "one of the best musical educations a fan could have" and giving Petty extra praise for choosing "to devote significant time and throw his passion into educating others on the radio about the music and traditions which influenced modern music."

The show meant a lot to Tom as well. "I love doing my 'Buried Treasure' show," he told the *Los Angeles Times*. "It keeps me listening like I used to do." He also enjoyed working with the new medium of satellite radio. "It's exciting because it's a new frontier in a lot of ways," he told *Gainesville Magazine*. "It reminds me a little bit of when MTV came along; they're eager for programming, and they're so open to ideas."

The show spun off two compilation albums, *Petty's Peculiar Picks: The Best of Tom Petty's Buried Treasure* (2014) and *More Petty's Peculiar Picks: The Best of Tom Petty's Buried Treasure Volume 2* (2015), in case you wanted to add some of Tom's favorite records to your own collection. Also in 2015, Tom got his own channel, when "Tom Petty Radio" debuted on SiriusXM on November 20, 2015.

By then, there hadn't been any new episodes of *Buried Treasure* aired since August 27, 2009. But after Petty's death, fans got a surprise bonus when three new episodes were broadcast in 2018. Tom had recorded the shows in November 2016; after his death, they were found by his producer/engineer Ryan Ulyate, who brought them to the attention of Tom Petty Radio's executive producer and host Mark Felsot.

The final shows aired on October 22, November 19, and December 17. It was great to hear Tom's voice again, as he played tracks like "Turn on Your Love Light" by Them, "Criminal" by Fiona Apple, and Presley's "Working on the Building." The final show, the 251st episode, opened with "Mary, Mary" by the Monkees and closed with what he called "a beautiful song"—"Got a Feelin'" by the Mamas and the Papas. And it was definitely a heartstring-pulling moment when he signed off with "I'll see you next week."

Buried Treasure reruns still air on Tom Petty Radio; members of Petty's official fan club can listen to the channel for free.

Tom does a radio phone-in in San Francisco in 1979, perhaps foreshadowing his future satellite radio gig. Tom loved sharing his extensive record collection on *Tom Petty's Buried Treasure*.

THE BIOGRAPHIES

CONVERSATIONS WITH TOM PETTY

TOM PETTY: THE BIOGRAPHY

NOVEMBER 2005

OCTOBER 2016

"Can everybody hear me?" Tom at the Sound Advice Amphitheater, West Palm Beach, Florida, on June 8, 2005.

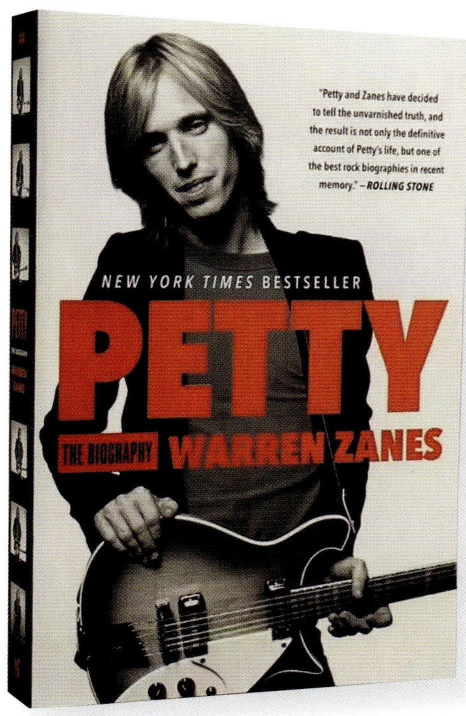

"This, to be sure, is not an autobiography," Tom writes in his forward to *Conversations with Tom Petty*. "That is for another book and another time." But his cooperation with two authors on their Petty books was so extensive they end up serving as de facto autobiographies anyway.

Consider the *Conversations* book. In its original edition, it ran more than 300 pages, and, being a series of Q&A interviews, the vast majority of the words are Tom's. Never again would he talk so extensively about his life and career. The original idea was that the book's focus would be on his music. But the more Petty and author Paul Zollo talked, the more apparent it became that his life had an enormous impact on his work. "So what started as a series of conversations about creativity and writing songs turned into really the story of his entire life," Zollo said in an interview with Canadian radio, "and he told me everything."

Zollo had known Petty since 1994. He was a musician himself, having been in LA band the Ghosters, as well as releasing solo albums; he was also a journalist who had held editorial positions at magazines such as *SongTalk* and *American Songwriter*. The two did a warm-up interview on March 31, 2004, which first appeared on Tom's website. Zollo then spent the next year sitting down for extensive talks with Petty at his Malibu home. Zollo not only probes into every corner of Tom's life (with the notable exception of his divorce), he also gets Tom to run down each of his albums (including compilations such as *Playback*), from *Tom Petty and the Heartbreakers* through *Highway Companion*.

It results in one of the most comprehensive looks at a musician's career, as told by that musician himself. As *Publisher's Weekly* wrote, "overall the book is successful because the notoriously media-wary Petty responds to Zollo's almost obsessive knowledge about his life, career and craft with articulate and intelligent answers that even nonfans can enjoy." The book was republished in expanded editions in 2020 and 2024.

Warren Zanes, author of *Petty: The Biography*, was also a musician; his band, the Del Fuegos, opened for the Heartbreakers in 1987. He also has a PhD, has taught at numerous universities, and serves as executive director of Steven Van Zandt's Rock and Roll Forever Foundation.

His 2003 book on Dusty Springfield's *Dusty in Memphis* album led Petty to get back in touch with him. Zanes would go on to edit the companion book for the *Runnin' Down a Dream* documentary. Eventually they spoke about Zanes writing a biography of Petty. Tom was clear about one thing: he didn't want it to be authorized. "He said he feels like when he sees that on the front top of the book, he knows it's going to be bullshit, an inside, white-washed account," Zanes told Boston radio station WBUR, "and he said, 'I want this to be your book. Not ghost-written, not cowritten, not authorized.'"

Which didn't mean that Petty always found it easy to go into areas Zanes wanted to explore. Tom resisted talking about his drug use, but he finally agreed to address the issue; he also discussed his divorce. Having Tom's cooperation also enabled Warren to get interviews with people close to Petty who had never been interviewed, such as roadie and guitar tech Alan "Bugs" Weidel. He also persuaded drummer Stan Lynch to open up about his troubled relationship with Petty.

Zanes' book received positive reviews, and it became a *New York Times* bestseller. "What I wanted was to capture the Tom Petty story and show how that story is the ideal case study if one wants to understand what the age of rock and roll meant in American life," Zanes said in an interview with *The Petty Archives* website.

59

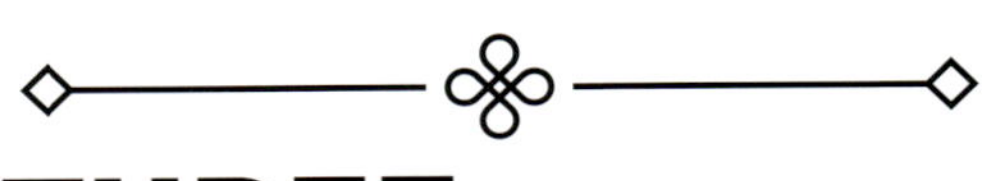

THREE DECADES AND COUNTING

THE THIRTIETH ANNIVERSARY TOUR

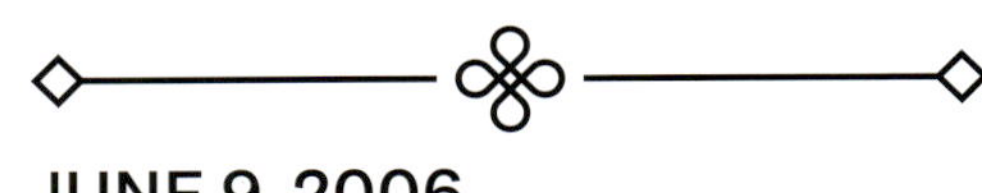

JUNE 9, 2006

Live in Atlanta, Georgia, on September 22, 2006, toward the end of the Heartbreakers' thirtieth anniversary tour.

It was shaping up to be a big year. In addition to Tom releasing a new solo album, the Heartbreakers would be celebrating their thirtieth anniversary with a coast-to-coast tour in 2006, including making a stop in the town where their story began, a place where they hadn't performed in thirteen years.

After opening in Charlotte, North Carolina, the five-month tour covered just about every corner of the United States, with a single date up north in Toronto, Ontario. The itinerary included festival dates: two appearances at Summerfest in Milwaukee, Wisconsin; a stop in Texas for the Austin City Limits Festival; and a headlining spot at the Bonnaroo Music and Arts festival on June 16 in Manchester, Tennessee. *Rolling Stone* called the Heartbreakers' set at Bonnaroo "a thrilling run of hits," with Petty as the jovial ringmaster: "He makes broad strumming gestures with his arms and kicks his legs, as if teaching a clinic on how to reach a huge crowd." On introducing surprise guest Stevie Nicks,

Portsmouth, Virginia, June 12, 2006. Stevie Nicks took advantage of every opportunity to perform with the Heartbreakers.

Curtain call in Atlanta, Georgia, on September 22, 2006.

who made appearances throughout the tour, Tom smiled as he teased the crowd, "I told you we were gonna have fun, didn't I?"

But the most memorable stop was always going to be in Tom's hometown of Gainesville, where the band played at the Stephen C. O'Connell Center on September 21. The band had last performed in the city on November 4, 1993, and Gainesville was ready to welcome them home. Mayor Pegeen Hanrahan officially proclaimed the day of the show "Tom Petty and the Heartbreakers Day," with every band member given a key to the city ("It's much nicer than Chicago's, I'll tell you that," Petty joked). Petty himself received an additional honor from the University of Florida: the UF Distinguished Achievement Award, for his accomplishments in music and his charity work. "I thank everybody," Petty said as he accepted the honor. "I thank the university for making us distinguished people."

The show that evening was a full-on celebration, Tom and the band taking

At the Hollywood Bowl on September 26, 2006.

the stage to a rousing ovation, the crowd then loudly singing along to the opening numbers, "Listen to Her Heart" and "Mary Jane's Last Dance." "What can I say?" Petty said after the latter number. "It's so great to be here. I really feel like I've come home." He got another cheer when he announced, "We have a long show for you tonight; I hope you paid the babysitter and everything."

The twenty-one-song set encompassed covers of Bo Diddley's "I'm a Man" and Them's "Mystic Eyes." There were obvious contenders like "I Won't Back Down" and "Refugee," and the unexpected inclusion of "Southern Accents," which Tom hadn't played live since 1993. "Maybe it was the giddiness of the hometown fans that spurred them on, or the joy of being home," wrote Leslie Streeter in the *Palm Beach Post*. "Maybe it was the presence of expert twirler and tambourine slinger Stevie Nicks. But Petty and the Heartbreakers were on fire, extending several of the songs in their more than two-hour show into jangly psychedelic free-for-alls, or into pumped-up blues symphonies." The show was later released as the concert film *Live from Gatorville* (and reissued as *Tom Petty and the Heartbreakers—From Gainesville: The 30th Anniversary Concert*).

Before the tour began, Tom hinted that it might be the band's last. He was well into his fifties now, and touring was becoming a little more tiring. But even he seemed to recognize that "[t]he band has somehow become bigger than all of us," as he told *Guitar Player*. "I see it in a kind of holy way. The Heartbreakers have made so many people happy that it would almost be a sacrilege to turn my back on it." And as it turned out, he had more than a decade of shows in front of him.

Xcel Energy Center, St. Paul, Minnesota, June 26, 2006. "All hail rock 'n' roll!" The thirtieth anniversary tour was a lovefest for band and audience alike.

"BOTH RETROSPECTIVE AND INTROSPECTIVE"

HIGHWAY COMPANION

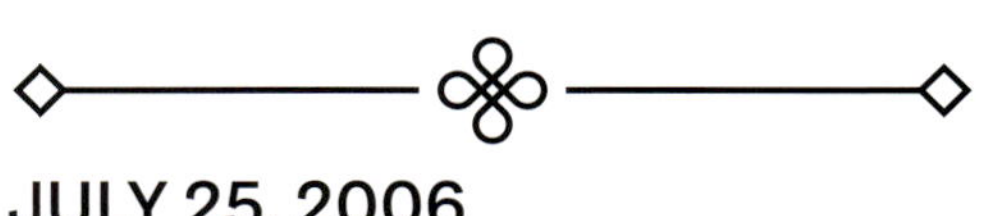

JULY 25, 2006

Highway Companion was Tom's last solo album, though as usual Mike Campbell was right by his side while making it. And so was Jeff Lynne, who coproduced the album along with Petty and Campbell.

Tom and Jeff had reconnected at George Harrison's posthumous induction into the Rock & Roll Hall of Fame. "The show went great," Tom told *Rolling Stone*, "and then we were coming back [to LA] on the plane and we said, 'Look, let's get together and cut a track.' That's how it always begins—with 'a track.'" Tom and Mike met up at Jeff's home to write songs, and when they had one completed, Jeff wanted to record it right away at his home studio. When Tom protested they didn't have a band, Jeff replied, "You play drums don't you?"

Thus the new project was set on the path to becoming a solo album. "That first track went really nice, so we just pitched camp at Jeff's studio," Tom explained to *Guitar Player*. "I kept dragging out songs, and the next thing we knew, we'd recorded ten tracks." He also enjoyed working with a stripped-down lineup of three people. "I just wanted the three of us to make a solo record," Tom said to *Rolling Stone*. "For this record, I'd rather bang it out myself and make a different kind of record."

As such, *Highway Companion* "steered away from anything that was too Heartbreakers sounding," as he told *Guitar Player*. "Early on, we decided not to use a lot of instrumentation. I kept saying to Jeff and Mike that I wanted it to sound like a combo. I wanted to leave a lot of space, and not try to fill everything in." Keyboards weren't used as much as on a Heartbreakers record, and Mike was asked to play so many parts on slide guitar

Two months after the release of *Highway Companion*, Tom takes the stage at the Hollywood Bowl on September 26, 2006.

he asked, "Do you really want slide again?" at one point. "There's slide on just about every number, but Mike was able to find enough tonal variations to produce lots of textures without the album sounding slickly produced," Tom explained.

He wanted the record to conjure up the feeling of the open road, telling *Mojo*, "I think the music is almost designed for America, because to me American music was all about listening to music in the car." Certainly the opening track, "Saving Grace," has him "flyin' over backyards" to a brisk beat. But other songs are more contemplative, like the downtrodden narrator of "This Old Town." The album's characters might have their freedom, but it seems to have left them at loose ends. Tom agreed there was a melancholy aspect of the album's "underlying theme of time and what it does to you. It makes you old, if you're lucky."

The album reached #4. "Saving Grace" was the only single to chart, cracking the Top 100 at #100, but reaching #26 in the Mainstream Rock Tracks chart. The iTunes release had a live version of "Saving Grace" as well as the song's video. And a special edition of the album released the following year featured four bonus tracks, including demo versions of "Big Weekend" and "This Old Town."

Though receiving some good reviews, the general consensus was that this was the weakest of Tom's three solo albums. For his part, Tom made it clear that chart success was not what he was aiming for, telling *Harp* magazine, "The biggest priority with the new record now is that I know this is here longer than me and that's more important than [it] being a hit record."

And he told *Rolling Stone*, "I am really proud of this record. I think it's one of my better ones in a long time."

61

"THE MOST FUN I'VE HAD IN YEARS"

THE RETURN OF MUDCRUTCH

AUGUST 2007

More than thirty years after Mudcrutch last worked together, Tom surprised everyone by reuniting the band. Here he leads the band in Santa Cruz, California, on April 14, 2008.

The making of *Runnin' Down a Dream* led to an event that nobody foresaw—a Mudcrutch reunion. But revisiting his past for the documentary led Tom to mull over the idea of getting the band back together. After all, Mudcrutch had never really had a good shot at showing what they could do, musically. Maybe now was the time.

When director Peter Bogdanovich interviewed guitarist Tom Leadon about the Mudcrutch era for the documentary, he mentioned, almost in passing, that Tom was thinking about a Mudcrutch reunion. The news hit Leadon "like a bolt of lightning," he recalled. He waited with baited breath until a phone call came from Petty himself, though he admitted he had to be convinced it was actually Tom on the line; after all, it had been three decades since they'd talked on the phone.

Randall Marsh was just as eager to get back behind the drum kit, and it was always going to be easy to get Mike Campbell and Benmont Tench on board. Actually, Leadon and Tench had never been in Mudcrutch at the same time. Nor was every previous member of Mudcrutch invited to the reunion, which led to some hurt feelings.

In August 2007, the newly revived band was in LA, ready to record Mudcrutch's first album. Despite not having played together for so long, the sessions went smoothly, the album recorded live with no overdubs. Tom even went back to playing bass. "The first day they came down we cut four tracks," Tom said to *Rolling Stone*. "It was like we never left. We're actually a lot better than we were then." Work on the record was completed in two weeks.

The album, simply entitled *Mudcrutch*, was released on April 29, 2008, and reached #8; the accompanying single, "Scare Easy," reached #4. *Entertainment Weekly* hailed the record as "the most classic-sounding and satisfying Tom Petty music since roughly the *Full Moon Fever* era," and other critics were just as enthusiastic. The album included some of the band's older material, such as "Queen of the Go-Go Girls" (a drawling country number about the band's days opening for strippers) and a few covers (such as the Byrds' "Lover of the Bayou"). But most of songs were new, and being recorded right after they were written gave the music a welcome dose of freshness. To hear the band in process of getting used to playing together again, listen to "Crystal River," a first take recorded on the first day of the sessions. Instead of editing it down (Petty: "We just couldn't bring ourselves to cut anything out"), it was released in its full length of nine minutes and thirty seconds.

A short tour of California was arranged to promote the album, which began April 12 in Malibu (a benefit performance for the LA-based Midnight Mission, an organization helping the homeless and others in crisis) and ran through May 2. A 4-track EP drawn from the tour, *Extended Play Live*, was released on November 11.

And that could've been the extent of it. But there was more to come. In 2015, the band was back with a new release, *Mudcrutch 2*, and a new tour, because "the first time was so much fun," Petty explained to *Uncut*. Seen as a more polished effort than its predecessor, the album rocked harder too, and this time the songs were all originals. *Mudcrutch 2* was released on May 20, 2016, and reached #10. Three days later, Mudcrutch began a twenty-date tour that extended all the way to the East Coast.

"It seemed like such a crazy idea that I figured something good would come out it," Petty explained to *Rolling Stone* about Mudcrutch's resurrection. But the real inspiration for the reunion was based on something more heartfelt: "I just started thinking about how I missed those guys."

Mike Campbell, not as a Heartbreaker but as a member of Mudcrutch. The band's reunion resulted in two albums and two tours.

Randall Marsh, back behind the drums in Mudcrutch.

Tom Leadon was excited when he heard Petty was considering reforming Mudcrutch and was quick to agree to join when Petty contacted him.

62

"A THOROUGH AND INFINITELY WATCHABLE PORTRAIT"

RUNNIN' DOWN A DREAM

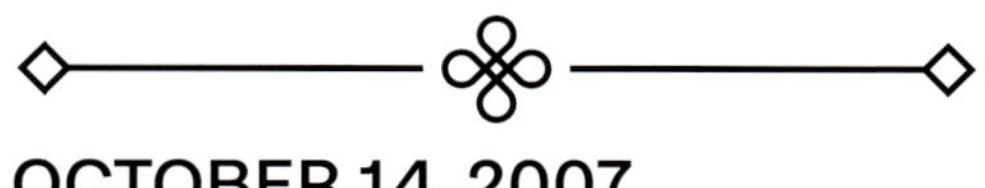

OCTOBER 14, 2007

Tom with *Runnin' Down a Dream* director Peter Bogdanovich.

As a band documentary, *Runnin' Down a Dream* was a remarkably comprehensive telling of the Heartbreakers story.

In 2005, director Peter Bogdanovich (*The Last Picture Show*, *Paper Moon*) was approached by George Drakoulias, who had started working with Petty on *Wallflowers* and eventually became his coproducer, about making a Heartbreakers documentary. Bogdanovich admitted he wasn't terribly familiar with the band. But after meeting with Petty, he decided to take on the project.

"The idea is to paint a collage, a picture of this group who came from Gainesville and what happened to them," Bogdanovich told *Billboard*. "The price you pay for fame and stardom—nothing is free. What is the price in terms of broken hearts and divorces and arguments and children and all that things that people go through? How do the private lives reflect the public and artistic lives?"

Bogdanovich had a wealth of material to work with. He spent the next two years going through the 400 hours of footage in the band's archives, then filmed an additional 100 hours of interview footage. Along with all the band members (including drummer Stan Lynch), there were also interviews with key business associates (manager Tony Dimitriades, producer Rick Rubin) and other performing artists Petty had worked with (Stevie Nicks, George Harrison, Dave Grohl).

Though he admitted he found it hard to open up in interviews, Tom nonetheless wanted the documentary to tell the band's story "completely."

Asked why the normally private Petty agreed to open up on camera about his career, Tom told journalist Melinda Newman, "I think it's a worthwhile project, and I think it's good that [Bogdanovich is] going to finally tell this story completely. He's put a lot of effort into it so far. Sometimes, giving up your privacy is a little like going to the dentist, and we have let him have access that no one's ever had. So far, it's looking good. We're all pretty excited about it. I think he's going to make a good movie."

Bogdanovich himself was pleased with the charisma of his primary subject, telling the *Gainesville Sun*, "I thought Tom would be good on camera and he is. He's very charming, very much himself and very honest."

The film's original cut ran to five hours; the final edit ran just under four hours. After opening with footage from the Heartbreakers' homecoming show in Gainesville in 2006, the film takes a chronological approach to the band's story. "We will be as candid as we can in the film," Bogdanovich told *Billboard*. "We want to explain what impact the group had on the world and the world on it. We will try to put their career into perspective, and we will really get into what Tom meant by his songs."

But while there's a lot of music featured in the film, Tom, with a few exceptions, doesn't talk too much about his songwriting—what inspires him, how the songs came into being. It's also interesting to note there's no mention of the *She's the One* soundtrack at all. Petty and company are open, but only to a point; there are no revelatory moments. But the film's length made it more than satisfactory to Petty fans.

The film had its premiere at the New York Film Festival. This was followed by one-night-only screenings in cities around North America (though it played two nights in Gainesville) with a screening on the Sundance Channel on October 29. There was a DVD/Blu-ray release as well, in both single-disc and four-disc editions. The film would also win a Grammy for Best Music Video, Long Form, in 2009.

Runnin' Down a Dream was warmly received, especially by Petty fans who loved the wealth of detail in the film. And Bogdanovich was pleased he'd been able to shine on a light on a musician he'd come to admire and respect: "He's just really a natural artist. He was born with it and figured out what to do with it at an early age. I mean, there's not another Tom Petty, you know?"

“GREAT, YET SIMPLE”

THE SUPER BOWL HALFTIME SHOW

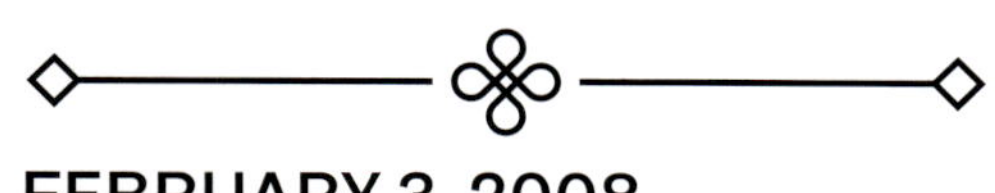

FEBRUARY 3, 2008

It was one of the Heartbreakers’ biggest audiences ever: an estimated 97.5 million. And it’s numbers like that which make playing a Super Bowl halftime show a highly prized gig, one which attracts music’s top performers who eagerly vie for landing the coveted spot.

The halftime show was once the realm of middle-of-the-road entertainment (college marching bands, mainstream performers such as Andy Williams and Carol Channing). But that changed in the 1990s, when efforts were made to attract a more youthful demographic, drawing in performers such as Aerosmith, No Doubt, and Prince.

Contenders to play Super Bowl XLII included Norah Jones and the Eagles. Tom Petty was also in the running, due to the success of the *Runnin’ Down a Dream* documentary. The final choice was announced on December 2, 2007: Tom Petty and the Heartbreakers got the nod. They were happy to accept. “We thought it was a great opportunity to play to a lot of people,” Tom said at a press conference prior to the game, “and it’s just a great event really; it’s a great American thing.”

The game was held at the University of Phoenix Stadium in Glendale, Arizona. Asked at the preshow press conference if, given the show’s size, they’d be playing more to the stadium audience or the viewing audience, he joked, “Well, a lot of it is just trying to remember the next chord!” He also admitted it was a challenge whittling his set down to a tight twelve minutes, saying they picked the songs they felt would work the best and “take you somewhere.” Asked about which team would win, he diplomatically demurred, “I don’t want to make a prediction on the game. I’m for everybody!”

The only “special effects” came at the beginning of the set, as the lights bordering the stage flashed on and off (the stage

incorporated both the shape of a guitar and a heart), with the pulsating sound of a heartbeat finally culminating in an explosion of pyrotechnics. The band was dressed down in black suits, accessorized by splashes of color; Petty wore a black scarf with white polka dots.

“American Girl” was an obvious opener, a song guaranteed to get the audience dancing and singing along. “I Won’t Back Down” was up next, a sentiment certainly appropriate to a sports competition. Tom spoke his first words to the crowd afterward as he changed guitars: “Thank you! God bless you, thank you!” Then came a quick “Free Fallin’,” with Tom, arms aloft, spinning around at the song’s end, taking in the spectacle. There was another quick “Thank you!” before the band kicked off with their last song, “Runnin’ Down a Dream.” It’s the most upbeat song in the set, with Petty finally getting a few moves in as he prowls the stage during the instrumental section. After another “Thank you so much!” the band stood together to take their final bow.

“It was fun,” wrote *Y! Sports* writer Frank Schwab. “You knew every song, and every word. It wasn’t a grandiose show like some halftime shows. It felt like Petty and the Heartbreakers just decided to show up and play a few songs for, oh, a hundred million people watching. It was upbeat.

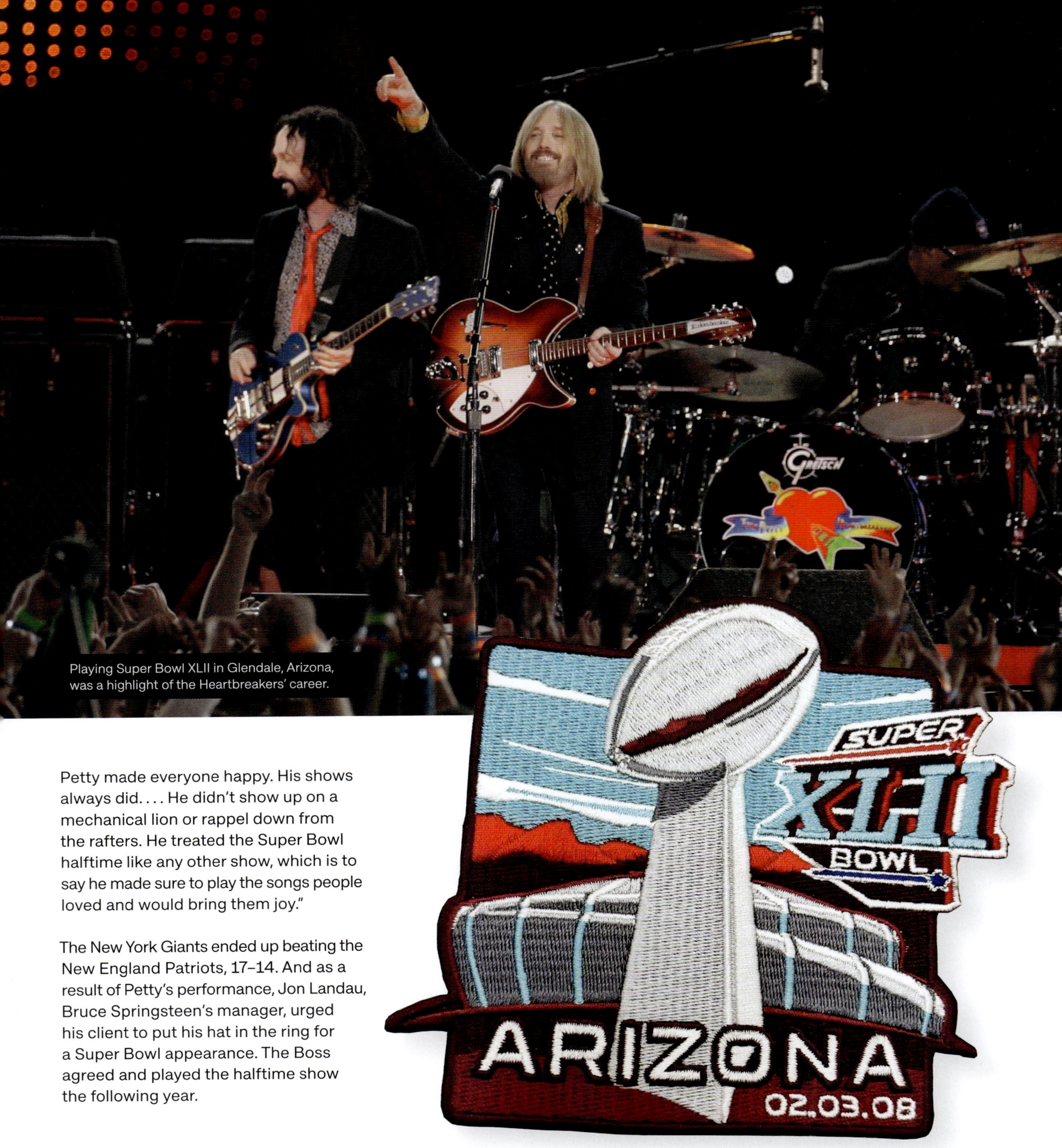

Playing Super Bowl XLII in Glendale, Arizona, was a highlight of the Heartbreakers' career.

Petty made everyone happy. His shows always did. . . . He didn't show up on a mechanical lion or rappel down from the rafters. He treated the Super Bowl halftime like any other show, which is to say he made sure to play the songs people loved and would bring them joy."

The New York Giants ended up beating the New England Patriots, 17–14. And as a result of Petty's performance, Jon Landau, Bruce Springsteen's manager, urged his client to put his hat in the ring for a Super Bowl appearance. The Boss agreed and played the halftime show the following year.

64

"ONE OF AMERICA'S PREMIER MUSIC ARTISTS"

THE LIVE ANTHOLOGY

NOVEMBER 23, 2009

Tom, seen here in 1980, had an impressive archive of live shows to draw on for *The Live Anthology*, as the band had been routinely recording their gigs from the beginning of their career.

Tom had released live albums before. But this was the kind of box set that makes a diehard fan's mouth water. Forty-eight tracks over four CDs, spanning the years from 1980 to 2007.

The Heartbreakers had previously put out two live releases—a promotional EP *Official Live 'Leg* (for "bootleg") in 1977, and *Pack Up the Plantation: Live!* in 1985. But the band had been recording their concerts for years. "Usually if we're going to be in a place for more than one day, if there were multiple shows, we'd say, 'Let's record this because we'll have time to get the sound really good,'" Tom explained to *USA Today*. "For whatever reason, we just hung on to anything that got recorded live, whether it was for a television show or [concert radio show] *The King Biscuit Flower Hour* or any number of things."

Which meant there was plenty of material to draw from when the set was being compiled. Ryan Ulyate, who had been working on Tom's records since 2003, put together an iTunes library of 170 Heartbreakers shows, featuring around 3,500 songs. At first, the thought of going through all that material seemed daunting. "I thought it would be a chore in a way," Tom told journalist Natalie Rotman. "I started to do it and I just fell in love with the project."

Tom worked with Mike Campbell, assessing the tracks that Ulyate chose to highlight. "It's amazing how the best take really shines compared to everything else," Tom observed about having to compare the numerous versions of a song like "Refugee." He also was pleased at how well he thought the performances held up: "I was surprised that we were as good as we were. I really didn't listen to us when we were back in our twenties and starting out. It was a really good little rock and roll band. I see why it caught on."

Poring over the recordings also brought memories of shows he'd rather forget, such as a 2007 benefit performance at the American Museum of Natural History. Petty told the *Wall Street Journal* it was "the worst gig," as he felt the attendees paid little attention to the band. Though he added, "At least I got a good track out of it," as the performance of "I Won't Back Down" chosen for the box set.

Tracks of special interest included live versions of songs the band never recorded in the studio: the high-powered "Drivin' Down to Georgia," the lovelorn "Surrender," the love song "Melinda" with its remarkable piano solo. There was also an impressive array of covers: the Byrds' "Ballad of Easy Rider," Bo Diddley's "Diddy Wah Diddy," and, most unexpectedly an instrumental version of the classic James Bond theme "Goldfinger" (though you do wish Tom had attempted a vocal).

The deluxe version of *Live Anthology* packed in a lot more material. A fifth CD with another 14 live tracks. An audio-only Blu-ray disc presenting all of the set's 62 tracks in high-resolution stereo and 5.1 surround sound, Tom equating the improved sound quality "to getting a color TV when you had only had black and white." Two DVDs, featuring the documentary *400 Days*, about the making of *Wildflowers*, and the band's 1978 New Year's Eve show at the Santa Monica Civic Auditorium. And a new vinyl pressing of the *Official Live 'Leg* promo EP. Plus a book with detailed liner notes and other memorabilia.

The set was hailed as presenting "a panoramic picture of the Heartbreakers' indestructible groove." For Petty, it reconfirmed his feelings about the Heartbreakers' legacy. As he says in the *400 Days* documentary, "There's really not more to us than what you see and what you hear. We're not trying to deliver any hidden messages. It's all really obvious. We're just trying to make good music."

"IT'S ESSENTIAL THAT THERE BE NEW THINGS"

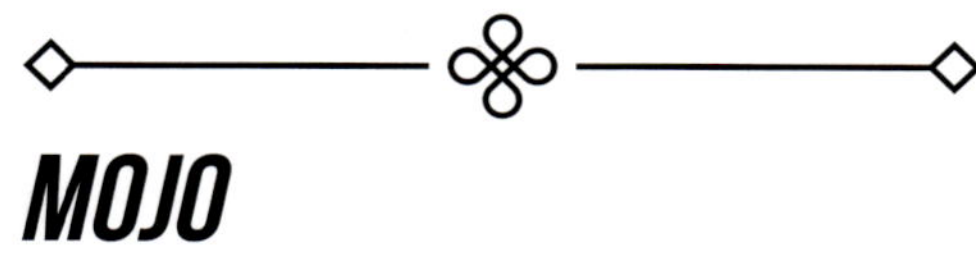

MOJO

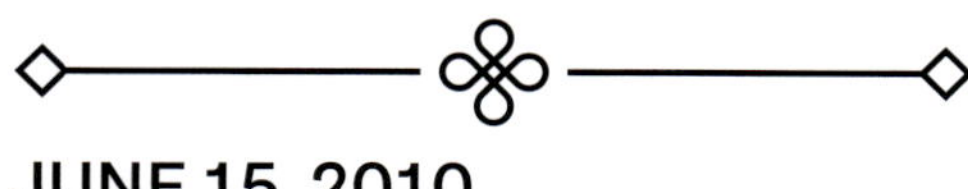

JUNE 15, 2010

It had been eight years since the Heartbreakers had made an album. Not that they'd been sitting around doing nothing. Some of the Heartbreakers had appeared on Tom's solo record *Highway Companion* and the Mudcrutch reunion album. And there was always another tour coming up. But now it was time for the Heartbreakers to get back into the studio.

In fact, the making of *Mudcrutch* ended up having a big influence in how *Mojo* was made. "I don't think I'd be here with the Heartbreakers if I hadn't done [*Mudcrutch*]," Tom told *Sound & Vision*. "Because it really opened my eyes up as how to really record!" The album had to be done in two weeks, as everybody had other commitments. "I had a couple of songs, maybe three, and we just had to whip them up and make it happen," Tom said. "The studio work went so well that I just thought, 'I can't possibly go back to any other way of working. It's too gratifying.' That was a real valuable musical lesson for me."

The band set up as if for a rehearsal. No baffles were used between the musicians. "I let things bleed a bit," Tom said, referring to, for example, a guitar amp microphone picking up the sound of another musician's instrument. "And no one wanted to play in headphones. That tends to cut you off. So I put floor monitors down like we would for a gig, those floor wedges. Not up very loud, because I didn't want them to bleed a lot."

The freewheeling atmosphere allowed the music to find its own direction. "There were a couple of songs that we would start playing and we'd get halfway through and look at each other and go, 'We've already covered this territory,'" Campbell told journalist Chris Willman. "We don't want to repeat ourselves." Tom relished the opportunity to play lead guitar on "Running Man's Bible." It also marked the first time engineer Ryan Ulyate received a coproducer's credit.

Musically, the *Chicago Tribune*'s Janine Schaults wrote that *Mojo* "lies somewhere between the British blues of John Mayall and the Southern sensibility of Jimmy Reed." Tom himself described it as the band's "warped way of making a blues record." There's certainly a blues sensibility running through tracks such as "First Flash of Freedom" and "The Trip to Pirate's Cove," but it's spiked with the feel of a modern rock band.

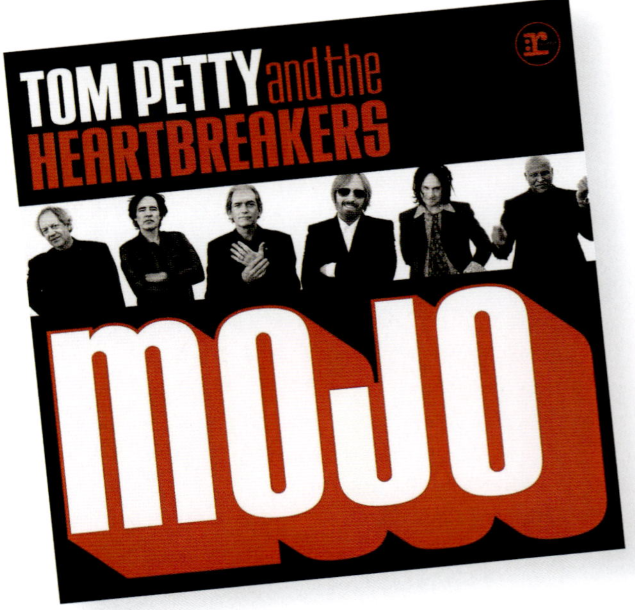

Tom in Denver, Colorado, in June 2010, the month *Mojo* was released.

Tom also noted there was "not a single note of harmony in the whole album—something I did on purpose," he told Willman. "It sounded too slick for the material. Now and then somebody would be sitting in the control room singing a harmony to something, and I'd go, 'Ah, nope, can't do it.'"

"This album sounds like the band sounds to me when it's after hours, when we're just playing and no one's really listening or paying attention," Tom concluded to journalist Mike Mettler. "That's when we're just playing for ourselves. And that was the sound I wanted to get."

The album reached #2. A few bonus tracks came out over the years; at the time of the album's release, "Little Girl Blues" was offered as an iTunes bonus track, and when *Mojo* was reissued in 2023, the song was again included as a bonus track on the digital version, along with "Mystery of Love" and a cover of Sonny Boy Williamson's "Help Me."

Billboard had given the album a good write-up: "It's not news that these guys rock, but on their first new album in eight years the Heartbreakers have their 'Mojo' working like they never have before—which is a fine thing indeed." Tom himself gave the record a more modest assessment. Asked by Willman what his hopes were for *Mojo*, he replied, "I'd like people to notice that we're still doing things that are worth hearing."

PART 5

END OF THE LINE, 2012–2023

On tour in 2014, the Moda Center in Portland, Oregon, on August 12.

Tom in London, June 2012, on the summer European tour.

"THE FANS DOUBTLESS COULDN'T ASK FOR MORE"

THE LAST EUROPEAN TOUR

JUNE 7, 2012

You could understand why Tom's European fans might feel neglected. He occasionally found time to do a show in London. But aside from one date in Hamburg, Germany, in 1999, Petty hadn't done a tour of the Continent since 1992.

That finally changed during his summer tour in 2012, which opened on April 19 in Broomfield, Colorado. After nine US dates and three Canadian shows, Petty and the Heartbreakers headed overseas, beginning with a June 7 date in Dublin. The critic for the *Irish Independent* called Tom the "laureate of off-beam Americana" and praised the show as "a return worth holding out for." The reviewer also enjoyed how the setlist went beyond a "greatest hits" format, mixing in "Curios songs such as the wigged-out 'It's Good to Be King' and a maraca-shaking version of Fleetwood Mac's 'Oh Well.'"

The European tour encompassed dates in Germany, Denmark, Sweden, Norway (for the Norwegian Wood festival), the Netherlands, France, Italy (the Heartbreakers' first-ever performance in the country), and three shows in England, including two nights at the Royal Albert Hall and a set at the Isle of Wight Festival.

Speaking with Neil McCormick from the *Daily Telegraph* about his excitement to be headed for the UK again, Petty reflected on his first tour of the country, when he opened for Nils Lofgren in 1977: "God, I had fun on that tour. I'm forever grateful, because it was off our success in England that we got a buzz going back home."

The shows at the Royal Albert Hall, on June 18 and 20, were especially meaningful to him, fulfilling a longtime dream of playing a full show at the legendary venue. Royal

Albert Hall had opened in 1871, and after decades of presenting more staid entertainment, it eventually played host to numerous rock acts. The Heartbreakers' previous appearance there had only been a short set during the Concert for George in 2002.

And Tom's UK fans were just as thrilled to see him. "As Petty's first gig in the UK since a mini-tour of Europe in 1999, this felt like a triumphant return to English soil," *Uncut* magazine wrote. "At one point, coincidentally or not, the lights hit Petty full on as he stood with his arms raised and outstretched; it causes the first of the night's many ovations." The *Guardian* critic similarly rhapsodized, "As he closes with his choicest anthem, 'American Girl'—a melody-slaked dash that's as perfect pop as rock 'n' roll ever gets—he makes this London landmark swing like a down-home Florida dive."

The second Royal Albert Hall show gave attendees a bit extra by featuring a special guest, Steve Winwood, who came on to join in on two songs by his former bands: Blind Faith's "Can't Find My Way Home" and the Spencer Davis Group's "Gimme Some Lovin'." The June 24 show in Amsterdam featured another special guest, when Pearl Jam lead singer Eddie Vedder turned up to help out on "The Waiting" and "American Girl."

In all, it was a successful, but too short tour, at least as far as the fans were concerned.

As an attendee who'd attended one of the Royal Albert Hall shows wrote on a music blog, "What a privilege and a joy it must be for someone like Petty to stand there in front of 5000 people and sing these amazing songs he has written over the past forty years. It was a privilege to be there, too."

The tour's last date was June 30 at the SAP Arena in Mannheim, Germany. Tom would go on three more tours with the Heartbreakers, and one with Mudcrutch, but he would never play a live date in Europe again.

After playing a short set at the "Concert for George," Tom was pleased to be able to play a full show at the same venue, the Royal Albert Hall, on June 18, 2012.

67

"URGENT AND COMMITTED"

HYPNOTIC EYE

Hypnotic Eye took two and a half years to complete, one of the longest gestations of any Heartbreakers album.

JULY 29, 2014

The Heartbreakers started work on their thirteenth album in August 2011. It wouldn't be finished for another two and a half years.

Part of that was because recording sessions were "made kind of in between tours," Tom explained to *Uncut*. The long gestation also led to a change in the musical tone: "The first few tracks were done two or three years ago. They were pretty hardcore blues tracks and really great, but then I started thinking, 'This is going down the same road twice—I'll hold onto those for later.' Then the songs just started determining how people were playing and the sounds they were getting. So at some point early on I started to think, 'Let's just do a real rock 'n' roll album.'" As he told the *Los Angeles Times*, "I don't like to make the same record twice."

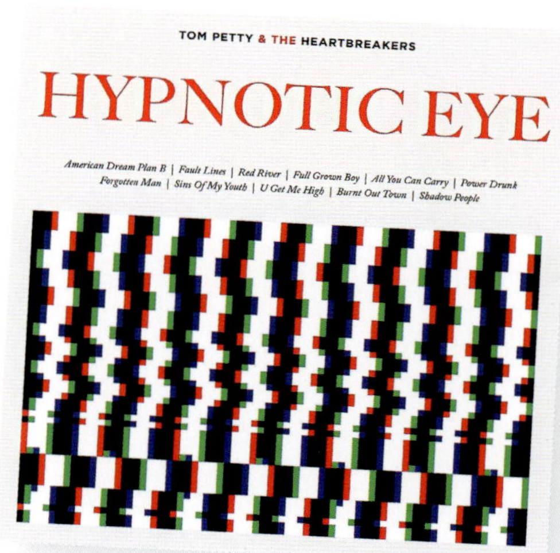

Which makes it interesting to compare those blusier numbers recorded earlier in the sessions, like the wistful, tentative love song "Full Grown Boy," with the punchier songs that were recorded later on, like "Red River," a portrait of a spooky "spirit queen." The songs the band worked on later also had some autobiographical elements. In 2007, wildfires threatened Tom's Malibu home. Twenty years after the arsonist's attack on his house in 1987, he must've felt like he was reliving a nightmare, watching as the flames consumed the buildings around him, finally grabbing a Hohner bass as he and his wife fled. This time, his house was spared. "All I Can Carry" was inspired by the incident, and there are references to fires in other songs as well.

But the album's main focus was social commentary. Tom described the record to *Billboard* as "a political album that's not really on either side," adding that it was "really more about morality than politics. It's about what's missing—why is the 'human' missing from humanity? I think the level of caring about other people is disappearing."

Such is the case in "Power Drunk," a taut number about how giving a man a little bit of authority (a badge in this instance) makes him start thinking "there's nothing out of his range." The strolling blues of "Burnt Out Town" underscores a devastating portrait of an urban wasteland. And the album's overarching theme can be found in its title (though interestingly, there is no title song).

"Hypnotic eye" refers to the devices that keep people mesmerized today—cell phones, televisions, computers—and how the misinformation conveyed by these devices eventually consumes the consumer. When Tom told *Billboard*, "The album is really about what the eyes are feeding [people] and how they are reacting to it," he might just as easily have been referring to the characters in "Shadow People," the evocative number that closes the album. And if Tom had no answers, he still felt it was important to ask questions. As he put to journalist Jason Anderson, "I can't save the world. I can only bitch about it!"

On its release, *Hypnotic Eye* drew positive comparisons with Petty's earlier work, reflecting "the crackling garage rock and taut underdog stories" on his first albums, as *Rolling Stone* put it. Tom agreed with such assessments, noting that what people were hearing was his "rock 'n' roll voice." None of the album's singles charted in the US. But *Hypnotic Eye* also did something that no other Petty album had done, topping *Billboard*'s main chart. For a music fan like Tom, finally getting his own chart topping album had to feel good.

And though no one realized it at the time, this turned out to be the last album released by Tom Petty and the Heartbreakers.

Tom and Mike Campbell in Raleigh, North Carolina on September 18, 2014, two months after the release of *Hypnotic Eye*.

"A DOWNRIGHT STUPID THING TO DO"

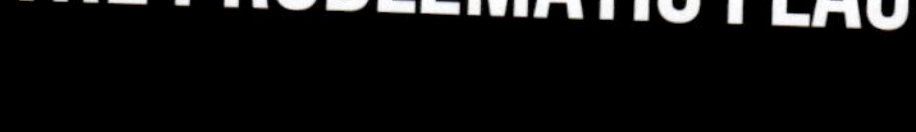

THE PROBLEMATIC FLAG

JULY 14, 2015

On June 17, 2015, Dylann Roof, a white supremacist, opened fire on a Bible study group at the Emanuel African Methodist Episcopal Church in Charleston, South Carolina, killing nine people and wounding one (Roof was later arrested and sentenced to death). In response, the South Carolina legislature passed a bill calling for the removal of the Confederate flag on the state capitol building. Governor Nikki Haley signed the bill, and the flag was lowered the following day.

The incident touched a nerve with Petty, who spoke to *Rolling Stone* about the issue in an article that ran in July, disavowing his own previous use of the flag. Confederate flag imagery had been used in the marketing of *Southern Accents*, including on tour, with the flag as part of the stage set. He felt the display of the flag provided some insight into the protagonist of the album's opening track, "Rebels," a man born "down in Dixie" who remains defiant in spite of his impoverished circumstances, which point to an ill-starred future; his "foot on the pedal" is matched by also having a foot in the grave.

But over time, Tom noticed that people seemed to think that his use of the flag meant that he also supported what the flag stood for. Things came to a head during a show in 1990, as described by journalist Fred Mills in an article for *Blurt* magazine. "A certain yahoo element had already been making its presence in the crowd known, emitting whoops and raising beer cups whenever Petty would make a regional reference," Mills wrote. "It was starting to feel like a NASCAR rally in the arena." And then someone threw a small, folded up item onto the stage. Mills described what happened next:

"Petty walked over, picked it up, and started unfolding it: a rebel flag, symbol of the Confederacy—and of a whole lot more. He froze, uncertain as to what he should do. *Well, wave it proudly at all your fellow Southerners*, you could almost hear the collective thought ripple through the air. Instead, Petty walked back to the mic, still holding the flag, and slowly began to speak, talking about how on the *Southern Accents* tour a few years ago they'd included a Confederate flag as part of

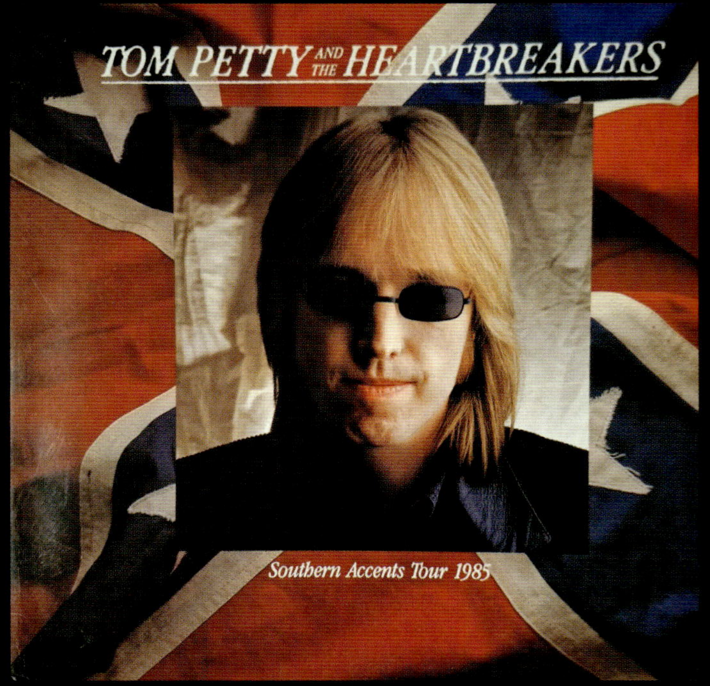

A program from the *Southern Accents* tour.

the stage set, but since then he'd been thinking about it and decided that it had been a mistake because he understood maybe it wasn't just a rebel image to some folks." Then, after declaring, "So we don't do this anymore," he crumpled up the flag, threw it back into the audience, and cued the band to start the next song.

There were some boos as well as cheers from the audience in response to his remarks, but Tom was relieved to find that people stopped bringing flags to his subsequent shows. He understood that some people regarded the flag as no more than "the wallpaper of the South," as he put it to *Rolling Stone*. Growing up, he'd seen the flag on a flagpole outside of the local courthouse, and it was regularly featured in popular culture, used by musicians ranging from Lynyrd Skynyrd to Billy Idol and seen on the roof of the car in the *Dukes of Hazzard* TV show.

Tom also revised the artwork for *Pack Up the Plantation: Live!* (1985), his first live album, seeing to it that a picture on the inside cover of the band playing in front of the flag was removed. It was all part of making amends. "It all stemmed from my trying to illustrate a character," he told *Rolling Stone*. "I then just let it get out of control as a marketing device for the record. It was dumb and it shouldn't have happened.

"People just need to think about how it looks to a black person," he added. "It's just awful. It's like how a swastika looks to a Jewish person. It just shouldn't be on flagpoles."

Tom, seen here around the time of *Southern Accents*, later came to regret his use of Confederate flag imagery on that tour, saying "It shouldn't have happened."

"I'M JUST REALLY HAVING FUN PLAYING"

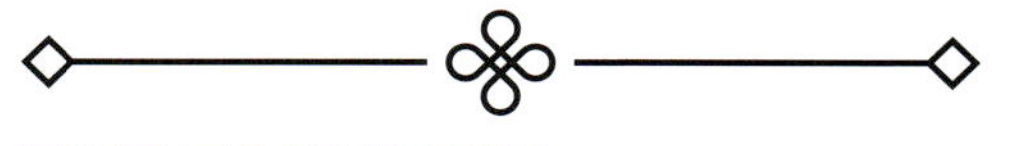

THE FORTIETH ANNIVERSARY TOUR BEGINS

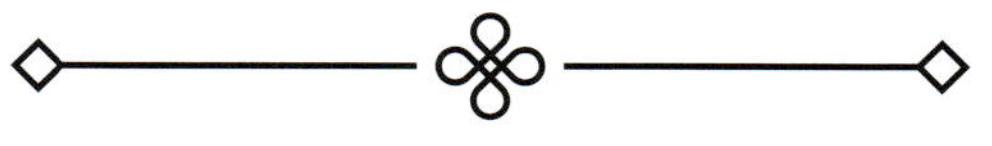

APRIL 20, 2017

Tom performs in London in 2017. Keeping a rock band together for forty years was certainly an accomplishment worth celebrating.

Five months. Three countries. Fifty-six concerts (including nine festival dates). And two vinyl box sets commemorating an impressive musical legacy (*The Complete Studio Albums Volume 1 [1976–1991]* and *The Complete Studio Albums Volume 2 [1994–2014]*). Tom Petty was celebrating his four decades in the music business in fine style.

The year opened with Tom being chosen as "Person of the Year" by MusiCares, a charity that provides financial support to people in the music industry. He was honored at a special benefit concert in Los Angeles on February 10 (which raised a record $8.5 million for the organization), featuring such performers as Randy Newman, Foo Fighters, Norah Jones, and Regina Spektor performing various Petty songs (Tom also played a forty-minute set himself).

Then it was time to prepare for the tour, the Heartbreakers' first since 2014. That tour had been promoting the Heartbreakers' most recent album, *Hypnotic Eye*; this tour was to be a celebration of the band's entire history. In addition to the main band—Petty, Mike Campbell (guitar), Ron Blair (bass), Benmont Tench (keyboards), Scott Thurston (guitar, keyboards, harmonica), and drummer Steve Ferrone—there were two backing singers, Charley and Hattie Webb, a British twosome more commonly known as the Webb Sisters.

The tour's opening date was in Oklahoma City, Oklahoma. The twenty-song set opened with "Rockin' Around (With You)" and closed with "American Girl." But there was no firm setlist. Tom had promised to mix it up by playing deep cuts along with the hits. He even threw in the Traveling Wilburys' "Handle With Care" at a few shows. "People ask me, 'What's your favorite song?'" he said during a show in Wichita, Kansas, by way of introducing "Have Love Will Travel" from *The Last DJ* album. "There isn't really an answer because there are so many. But this is one of my favorite ones. It's not a well-known one or anything, but I'm going to play it because I feel like playing it." It added a freewheeling element to the shows that the fans loved.

There were the usual bumps along the way. During rehearsals, Tom fell and ended up with a hairline fracture in his hip, which would give him problems throughout the tour. Dates in Berkeley and Sacramento had to be rescheduled when Tom became ill with laryngitis. A thunderstorm during an outdoor show in Morrison, Colorado, led to the performance being halted until the storm had passed. The band ended up playing past the curfew on the opening night of their Hollywood Bowl engagement and ended up getting fined $5,000.

But by and large, the concerts were "love fests," as Brian Q. Newcomb wrote of the show in St. Louis. That night, Tom had promised a "One hundred percent rock show! No artificial sweeteners, no corporate sponsors. This show is brought to you by you," and the fans responded in kind, often singing along "in a volume to match the band," as Newcomb wrote (he also noted that during "You Don't Know How It Feels" there was "at least one person somewhere behind our seats who took that line about 'rolling another joint' as an invitation"). There were occasional special guests too, including Stevie Nicks, who sang on "Stop Draggin' My Heart Around" at the band's sole date in the UK, at London's Hyde Park.

In *Forbes*, Steve Baltin wrote that while anniversary tours "can often feel phoned in or like money grabs," Petty's shows "felt like an opportunity to see a rejuvenated artist that is fully enjoying his role as a rock icon." It was an assessment Tom agreed with. "I've really enjoyed being onstage so much this tour," he told *Rolling Stone*. "I don't know exactly why, but it's so much fun, you know?"

On stage in Milwaukee, Wisconsin, on July 6, 2017. As always, Mike Campbell is right by Tom's side

Gibson
GRETSCH
HEARTBREAKERS

"IT WAS A JOY"

Producing Chris Hillman's *Bidin' My Time* was Tom's last studio project.

PRODUCING CHRIS HILLMAN'S *BIDIN' MY TIME*

SEPTEMBER 22, 2017

One of Tom Petty's last musical projects didn't involve making a record himself. It was serving as the producer for Chris Hillman's album *Bidin' My Time*.

Chris Hillman had a storied history. He first found fame as a founding member of the Byrds and played a key role in the development of country-rock, both on the Byrds' *Sweetheart of the Rodeo* album (1968) and as a founding member of the Flying Burrito Brothers. His biggest post-Byrds success came with the Desert Rose Band, who landed a number of singles on the country charts.

But after the release of his solo album, *The Other Side*, in 2005, he left studio life behind. "I didn't think I would ever make another record," he told *Billboard*. "I was sort of winding down. It was, 'OK, I've had a great 54-year career"; he was happy with what he'd already achieved. Then, events conspired to change his mind.

His Desert Rose Band cofounder Herb Pedersen had played on *Mudcrutch 2*, the second album released by Mudcrutch in 2016, after which he was invited to go on tour with Petty. Mutual acquaintances suggested Pedersen and Petty produce an album for Hillman, and Hillman was encouraged to give Petty a call. Chris hadn't spoken to Tom since January 1989, when Petty had joined the Byrds at a reunion show that month in Ventura, California. But he made the call, and Tom loved the idea of working with Chris, immediately offering the use of his studio. "You haven't even heard some of the songs," Hillman pointed out. "I'm not worried," Petty replied. "Well, I'd be worried because I don't know if they're that good!" Hillman responded.

Despite Hillman's initial reservations, the sessions, which began in 2017, went smoothly, Hillman calling working with Petty "just the stimulus for creativity that I needed." The plan was to make an acoustic album, but that changed as the sessions progressed, and the occasional electric guitar was allowed in. A number of Hillman's musician friends made appearances on the record. Herb Pedersen was an obvious choice. Some of Hillman's fellow Byrds could also be found, David Crosby providing harmonies on "Bells of Rhymney" and Roger McGuinn playing electric guitar on the first ever studio version of the Byrds song "Here She Comes Again" (the song had previously only been performed live). And members of the Heartbreakers also turned up.

Tom plays harmonica on "Given All I Can See," but he mostly stayed focused on his role as a producer. He made some valuable suggestions. When he heard Hillman and Pedersen jamming on the Everly Brothers' "Walk Right Back" between songs, he rushed out of the booth to say, "That sounds so good! We *have* to record it right now." It duly became an album track. When Petty was honored as MusiCare's "Person of the Year," he invited Hillman and Pedersen to perform his song "Wildflowers" at the charity organization's ceremony honoring him. The performance went so well that they decided to record a version for the album.

When Chris thanked Tom at the end of sessions, saying this was probably going to be his last album, Petty was quick to say, "What are you talking about? I'm not done with you yet." Future work together was a strong possibility, maybe even a Byrds reunion. "If anyone could have gotten us into the studio to do an album, it would have been Tom Petty," Hillman said in his memoir, *Time Between*. Those plans ended with Petty's death. Instead, Hillman has his memories of "a kind and very humble man who took me under his wing for that brief time in early 2017 to produce the best solo record of my career."

Tom had such a good time working with Chris Hillman he suggested they work on another album together.

"IT WAS MAGICAL"

THE LAST SHOW

SEPTEMBER 25, 2017

The Heartbreakers' fortieth anniversary tour wrapped up with three nights at the Hollywood Bowl, with shows on September 21 and 22, and, after two days off, a final show on September 25. Every concert was a sellout. The *Los Angeles Times* called it a "triumphant stand."

Lucinda Williams was the opening act for the three shows. After finishing her set for the September 25 show, she dropped into Tom's dressing room. "He had a big smile, and he was putting a cough drop into his mouth," she recalled. "Tom, the audience is rockin'," she told him. "They're good to go. I've warmed them up for you." "I bet you did," he replied, and the two hugged. It was the last time Williams would see her longtime friend.

"Petty covered every mile of his journey with determined, jubilant force," *Rolling Stone* wrote of the final show, "his creative odyssey as a songwriter; the commercial success that continually followed him; the record-business trials that came along with it; his eternal garage-band bond with the Heartbreakers." The eighteen-song set went right back to the beginning with the standard opener, "Rockin' Around (With You)," from the Heartbreakers' debut album. He also referenced the past when he dedicated "I Won't Back Down" to Jon Scott, the ABC Records promotions rep who'd got radio play for "Breakdown" all those years ago in 1976: "He went to the radio stations with a vengeance and brought that sucker onto the charts. And it wasn't easy. We're forever grateful." Perhaps that's what inspired him to add "Breakdown" to this evening's set, replacing "Walls," which had been played at the other Hollywood Bowl shows.

The main set concluded with "Runnin' Down a Dream." But in contrast to the rest of the tour, the Hollywood Bowl shows featured two songs during the encore. First up was "You Wreck Me," from *Wildflowers*. "I want to thank all of you for coming out tonight and celebrating!" Tom said after playing the song on

September 25. "We love you dearly. I want to thank you for 40 years of a really great time. We're almost out of time. We got time for this one . . ." And what else could it be but "American Girl," the longtime live favorite that invariably became a crowd singalong, bringing the show to a celebratory close.

Reviews made it clear what a much-loved performer Tom was. "Petty remains the perfect combination of an everyman who is One of Us and a rock superstar definitely not One of Us," *Variety* wrote. "He's won us over without ever seeming like he's trying to, which maybe is one factor in why America isn't any more tired of him and his Cheshire grin in 2017 than we were in a pre-MTV era."

A few days later, Tom sat down with Randy Lewis of the *Los Angeles Times*. "This year has been a wonderful year for us," he told Lewis. "This has been that big slap on the back we never got." Though admitting it was time to take a break ("I just have to learn to rest a little bit, like everyone's telling me"), he made it clear he intended to keep working ("I like to get out of bed and have a purpose"). He talked enthusiastically about producing LA band the Shelters' second album (he'd coproduced their first). And though he admitted age would surely slow down the pace of touring, there was no indication the Heartbreakers would be retiring any time soon.

There was certainly incentive to go back out on the road; the fortieth anniversary tour had grossed $61 million. As Benmont Tench told *Rolling Stone*, "I figured I'd get a call in a month or two: 'Tom wants to get together and jam some shit out.'"

Petty rocks the Del Mar Racetrack and Fairgrounds in San Diego, California, the week before his final shows at the Hollywood Bowl.

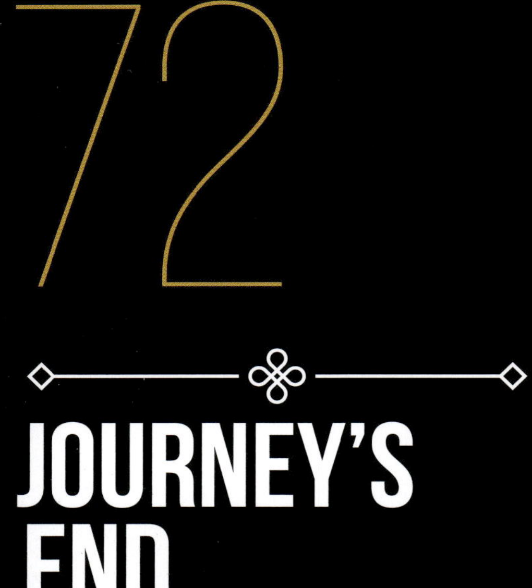

JOURNEY'S END

THE DEATH OF TOM PETTY

OCTOBER 2, 2017

It was a shocking end, because it was so sudden and unexpected.

Just over a week after the Heartbreakers' 2017 tour had ended, Tom was found unconscious at his Malibu home. He was rushed to UCLA Medical Center, but died later that day. He was sixty-six years old.

Initially, it was announced that Petty's death was due to cardiac arrest. But the medical examiner's report revealed a harsher truth, attributing his death to "multisystem organ failure due to resuscitated cardiopulmonary arrest due to mixed drug toxicity." In other words, a deadly combination of drugs, which the report also listed: fentanyl, acetyl fentanyl, despropionyl fentanyl and oxycodone (opioids), temazepam and alprazolam (sedatives), citalopram (an antidepressant).

Given Petty's previous issues with drugs, some might have wondered if he had relapsed. But it was quickly established that Tom was taking medications for a variety of ailments, and that he had been in constant pain due to the hairline fracture resulting from the fall he'd had while rehearsing for the tour.

Throughout the recent tour, Tom's bandmates could see the difficulties the fracture was causing him. Drummer Steve Ferrone would help him get on stage every night, letting Tom put his arm around his shoulder as they climbed the stairs to the stage. "I'd say, 'How are you doing? You ready for the show?'" Ferrone told *Rolling Stone*. "He'd say, 'Just get me up there and I'll be OK.'" But Tom gave no thought to canceling the tour. As his wife Dana later told the *Los Angeles Times*, "He was very stubborn. His feeling was, 'I can't do that to my crew. I can't do that to the fans. I can't do that to my band.'"

After the tour, Tom learned that the hairline fracture had now become a full break and that he would require hip surgery. But he'd just come off the road and didn't want to deal with it right away. He could always schedule the surgery for later. In the meantime, he continued to curb his pain with medications—which, sadly, resulted in his death.

"We knew before the [medical examiner's] report was shared with us that he was prescribed various pain medications for a multitude of issues including Fentanyl patches," Petty's family said in a statement, "and we feel confident this was, as the coroner found, an unfortunate accident.... Many people who overdose begin with a legitimate injury or simply do not understand the potency and deadly nature of these medications." Tom also had other health issues, including knee problems, emphysema, and coronary artery atherosclerosis.

When his death was announced, tributes arrived quickly. "It's shocking, crushing news," said Bob Dylan in a statement. "I thought the world of Tom. He was a great performer, full of the light, a friend, and I'll never forget him." "God bless Tom Petty," tweeted Ringo Starr. "Peace and love to his family. I'm sure going to miss you Tom." Cameron Crowe's tribute was short and sweet: "No words. Just thanks." Tom's star on Hollywood Boulevard was soon covered with candles and flowers. Fans from the self-proclaimed Tom Petty Nation headed for Gainesville to celebrate what would've been his sixty-seventh birthday at the first Tom Petty Weekend (an event still being held at the time of this writing).

In the meantime, the family tried to find solace amongst the tragedy: "On a positive note we now know for certain he went painlessly and beautifully exhausted after doing what he loved the most, for one last time, performing live with his unmatchable rock band for his loyal fans on the biggest tour of his 40-plus year career. He was extremely proud of that achievement in the days before he passed." And now the work would begin on keeping Tom Petty's legacy alive.

Tom performs with the Heartbreakers in Toronto in 2017. His death later that year shocked and saddened fans—and the music world at large.

73

"TURNS SADNESS INTO JOY"

AN AMERICAN TREASURE

SEPTEMBER 28, 2018

An American Treasure celebrated Tom's musical legacy.

Just months after her father's death, Tom's eldest daughter Adria Petty began work on what would be his first posthumous release. At first, it seemed like she might have taken on too much, too soon. But, as she later told *CBS This Morning*, "I guess I just felt like putting our energy and our grief into something positive was a better thing than just twisting in the wind for a year."

That didn't mean it was going to be easy. Adria wasn't working alone; Tom's widow, Dana, Heartbreakers Mike Campbell and Benmont Tench, and producer/engineer Ryan Ulyate were all involved in sorting through the archives. As Adria told CBS, at times their mutual grief was overwhelming. "It was absolutely awful for all of us. At different stages, different ones of us couldn't participate," she said. "But it's something that you have to do, in service to the art and the man."

The group also took a different approach in compiling the setlist. "We hadn't put out a greatest hits for a while," Tench told *Entertainment Weekly*. "We put out a live anthology and a lot of live recordings because we've always felt we were better live. But the thing is that this is obviously to pay tribute to Tom. We know that *you* know this is special. But do you know how special that stuff was on records that you may have missed? And there are different versions of songs that may be subtly different or drastically different that might make you take another look at them."

The songs went all the way back to days of Mudcrutch. "Lost in Your Eyes" was recorded in Tulsa in 1974, with a little help from members of the Texas swing band Alvin Crow and the Pleasant Valley Boys, who added harmonica and fiddle. "Tom is a rock and roll singer, but this song is Otis Redding," Campbell told *Variety* of the song. "He was a soul singer, too. When he hits that high note—pure soul."

There was also the chance to rescue songs that might otherwise have slipped through the cracks for good. Campbell was thrilled when "Lonesome Dave," recorded during the same sessions as "Mary Jane's Last Dance," was resurrected. The rollicking track gleefully taps into the spirit of Chuck Berry and was hailed by *Variety* as "one of the most fun things the Heartbreakers ever recorded."

Most of the tracks were presented as is, but a few new overdubs were added. "Surrender" was a song the Heartbreakers had recorded in their early days but never felt entirely happy with. A new mix and new guitar solo finished the job. "We didn't mess with stuff too much like that," said Tench. "I think there may be one or two cases where we went, 'This needs guitar,' and you just add like eight bars in the middle because there was going to be a solo. But we didn't go back and fix this and change that and massively rework stuff."

Adria gave the release its title: "I was the one that was like, 'Let's call it *An American Treasure* because he was one." There were two versions of the set, a standard two-CD edition and deluxe four-CD edition (and their vinyl equivalents), with most tracks being previously unreleased. Adria also directed the videos for "Keep a Little Soul" and "You and Me."

And Tench's comments about the set undoubtedly expressed the feelings of everyone who had worked on it: "To put this box set together for me wasn't just cathartic: It just was kind of validating. Just, like, 'Yes, he was as good as I thought he was, and better. Yes, we were a really good band.' But also you hear the guy counting this song off, or going, 'That was really good.' You hear all the chatter and everything and it keeps it alive in your heart. And it was a good experience for me to do this."

CEASE AND DESIST

NO PRESIDENTIAL USAGE ALLOWED

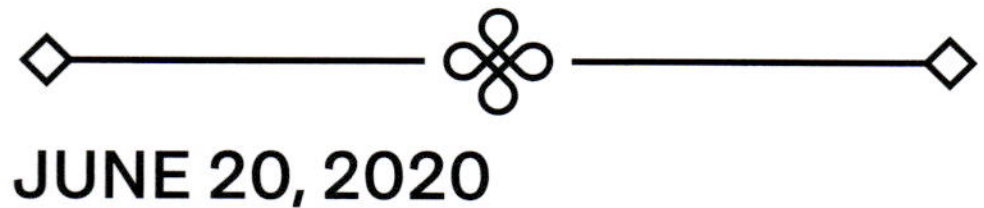

JUNE 20, 2020

It was the day of President Trump's campaign rally in Tulsa, Oklahoma. Among the music played during the event was the stirring rallying cry of "I Won't Back Down."

The Petty family was not amused.

"Trump was in no way authorized to use this song to further a campaign that leaves too many Americans and common sense behind," the official Tom Petty account tweeted the same day as soon as they learned about the incident. "Both the late Tom Petty and his family firmly stand against racism and discrimination of any kind. Tom Petty would never want a song of his used for a campaign of hate. He liked to bring people together.... We would hate for fans that are marginalized by this administration to think we were complicit in this usage. Concurrently, we have issued an official cease and desist notice to the Trump campaign." The statement was signed by Petty's daughters Adria and Annakim, his first wife Jane, and his widow Dana.

The Petty family wasn't alone in complaining about the Trump campaign wrongfully appropriating an artist's music; Tom is listed as one of the more than forty acts mentioned on the "Musicians who oppose Donald Trump's use of their music" page on Wikipedia. And when Tom was alive, he'd objected to George W. Bush using the song in his own presidential campaign in 2000— which itself inspired the comedy show *Veep* to have a plot line about the character Jonah Ryan (Timothy Simons) running for Congress that drew on the incident. When he's told Petty doesn't want him using "I Won't Back Down" anymore, Ryan snaps back, "Well, fuck him if he thinks I'm going to back down! That's, like, the whole point of the song!"

It's a point of contention that resurfaces during every major election season in the US. And whether a politician can use an artist's song is not necessarily a clear cut matter. In an article in the *Guardian*, Ben Depoorter, a professor at University of California Law San Francisco, explained that many venues have licenses with performing rights companies such as ASCAP and BMI, who oversee the use of music by the artists they handle, meaning the venues can play whatever music they like. The situation becomes more complicated when a third party, like a candidate, is involved; then political campaigns need to get their own music licenses. "When these authors are saying, 'Hey, I don't want him to play my music any more,' it's actually a legal right they have," Depoorter explained.

Tom paid attention to who was using his songs, and for what purpose. In 2008, he let Hillary Clinton use "American Girl" during her bid for president. But in 2011, he fired off a cease-and-desist letter when Michele Bachmann used the same song during her own short-lived campaign for president. The Petty estate has been just as vigilant since his death. Despite the fact that Tom, and his estate, made it clear there was no interest in supporting Republican candidates, in 2022 Kari Lake nonetheless used "I Won't Back Down" in a video montage when she contested the results in Arizona's governor's race. The Petty estate was quick to respond, saying the song had been "stolen and used without permission or a license to promote Kari Lake's failed campaign..... We are exploring all of our legal options to stop this unauthorized use and to prohibit future misappropriations of Tom's beloved anthem." A cease-and-desist order duly followed.

And less than a year later, the Trump clan seemingly got around the request to cease-and-desist. Lara Trump, married to Trump's son Eric, recorded her own, country-influenced version of "I Won't Back Down," in September 2023. The song reached the Top 10 on *Billboard*'s Digital Song Sales chart—but it didn't turn up at any campaign rallies.

Tom had strong opinions about which politicians could make use of his songs during their campaigns.

75

A B-SIDE RESURRECTED

THE MUSIC LIVES ON

DECEMBER 4, 2023

"American Girl" was the first Heartbreakers song to appear in a film; *Fast Times at Ridgemont High*.

The video game wasn't set to be released for another two years. But when the trailer for *Grand Theft Auto VI* came out at the end of 2023, featuring Petty's "Love Is a Long Road," it sent streams of the song on Spotify through the roof. Was this an indication of how Tom's music would be promoted in the coming years?

After Tom's death, his estate had overseen the release of compilations such as *An American Treasure* and *The Best of Everything*. Releases were then put on hold due to a legal battle between Petty's two daughters and his widow over control of the estate. Fortunately, matters were soon resolved, and the Tom Petty Legacy LLC was established "to manage all aspects of Tom's legacy," according to a joint statement. "We are committed to honoring Tom's voice, music, integrity and his charitable spirit.... The business will build upon Tom's 40+ years of great music and his historic career."

In the era of streaming and downloads, placing songs in TV shows, films, and even ads had been an increasingly important revenue stream for recording artists. Tom's music had been regularly featured in films and TV shows since "American Girl" appeared in *Fast Times at Ridgemont High* in 1982. His music had also been featured in such video games as *Rock Band 2* and *4*, *Guitar Hero 5*, and *Rocksmith 2014*.

"Runnin' Down a Dream" was used in *Grand Theft Auto: San Andreas* (2004).

"Love Is a Long Road" was a long-forgotten B-side until it was used in the trailer for the video game *Grand Theft Auto VI*.

And nine years later another song from the same album (*Full Moon Fever*) was picked for the trailer for the much-anticipated *Grand Theft Auto VI* (*Grand Theft Auto V*, released in 2013, had sold over 190 million copies).

"Love Is a Long Road" matches an upbeat rock melody with bittersweet lyrics; this is a relationship doomed to failure. It was only released on a single as the B-side of "Free Fallin'" in the UK, though it got enough US radio play to reach #7 in *Billboard*'s Mainstream Rock Tracks chart. Use of the song in the *GTA6* trailer provided a time warp back to the '80s. "Hearing Petty's characteristic moan in this trailer filled me with the same sense of nostalgia that I get when I swing by my parents' house and hear my dad strumming his guitar in the basement," wrote Maddy Myers on the *Polygon* website. "And that's kinda how I feel about returning to the world of Grand Theft Auto, so… sure." A couple of "Easter eggs" were dropped into the video for sharp-eyed Petty fans as well; in one scene, a sticker can be seen on a door that reads "Petty Forever."

Views for the trailer on YouTube took off, surpassing 100 million views in two days; at the time of this writing, that had increased to over 200 million views. People then began seeking out the trailer's song itself. Prior to the trailer's release, "Love Is a Long Road" had around 5 million streams on Spotify. But the excitement generated by the trailer led to a rapid increase in streams of the song, taking it up to 40 million streams. It was enough to send the song back into the *Billboard* charts, where it peaked at #7 in the magazine's US Rock Digital Song Sales chart. At the time of writing, *GTA6* was scheduled to be released in the fall of 2025.

And that's as good a sign as any of the staying power of Tom Petty's musical legacy. With songs that continue to resonate with generation after generation, and ever-changing formats in which to hear those songs, we'll be listening to Tom Petty's music for decades to come.

Tom on his last tour in Toronto, on July 15, 2017.
Though his voice is silent, his music lives on.

BIBLIOGRAPHY

ARTICLES

"100 Greatest Artists." *Rolling Stone*, December 3, 2010.

Abbott, Jim. "Petty Strikes Gold By Panning Greed Of The Music Biz." *Orlando Sentinel*, October 8, 2002.

Anderson, Jason. "I'm Not Mr. Laidback!" *Uncut*, September 2014.

Baltin, Steve. "How Tom Petty Ruled Classic Rock With The Tour Of 2017." *Forbes*, September 25, 2017.

Banas, Erica. "9/11: 5 Inspiring Concert Tributes." 957benfm.com, September 11, 2023.

Benitez-Eves, Tina. "Behind the 2017 Death of Tom Petty." *American Songwriter*, October 2, 2023.

Beviglia, Jim. "Behind The Song: Tom Petty, 'Free Fallin'.'" *American Songwriter*, 2020.

Block, Melissa. "Tom Petty On Cheap Speakers And George Harrison." *All Things Considered*, NPR, August 4, 2014.

Block, Melissa. "'A Song For Any Struggle': Tom Petty's 'I Won't Back Down' Is An Anthem of Resolve." *All Things Considered*, NPR, May 8, 2019.

Bonner, Michael. "Tom Petty: Royal Albert Hall, London, June 18." *Uncut*, June 19, 2012.

Browne, David. "Music Reviews: 'Wildflowers' and 'You Got Lucky.'" *Entertainment Weekly*, November 4, 1994.

"Three Years After Tom Petty's Death, His Dream Project Finally Emerges." *Rolling Stone*, September 16, 2020.

Cantor, Matthew. "'Please let me get what I want': can artists stop politicians from using their songs?" *The Guardian*, January 30, 2024.

Chelin, Pamela. "Let Your Heart Be Your Guide: Adria Petty, Mike Campbell & More On The Enduring Significance Of Tom Petty's 'Wildflowers.'" Grammy.com, October 16, 2020.

Chick, Stevie. "Tom Petty and the Heartbreakers-review." *The Guardian*, June 19, 2012.

Cohen, Finn. "The Day Prince's Guitar Wept the Loudest." *The New York Times*, April 28, 2016.

Collis, Clark. "Dave Grohl Q&A: The Foo Fighters frontman talks about the new Foos album, saying no to 'Glee,' and playing 'Smells Like Teen Spirit for the first time in 18 years." *Entertainment Weekly*, August 4, 2017.

"Conversations with Tom Petty" (review). *Publisher's Weekly*, 2005.

Corcoran, Michael. "Raised on Promises." *Spin*, August 1989.

Crandall, Bill. "TP2 . . . This Time It's Personal." *BAM*, February 7, 1997.

Daly, Mike. "Tom Petty, Rock's Elite." *Melbourne Age*, June 25, 1987.

"*Damn the Torpedoes*: Review." *Orange Coast Magazine*, January 1980.

Dean, Bill. "Petty's odyssey: Film shines light on artist, his Gainesville roots." *The Gainesville Sun*, October 14, 2007.

DeCurtis, Anthony. "Tom Petty's new LP: Back to basics." *Rolling Stone*, May 7, 1987.

DeYoung, Bill. "On Record: Wilburys: Unassuming and fun." *The Gainesville Sun*, October 28, 1988.

"Tom Petty presents a solo album." *The Gainesville Sun*, April 26, 1989.

DiMartino, Dave. "Into the Great Wide Open." *Entertainment Weekly*, July 19, 1991.

Donkeypong. "Tom Petty's 'Buried Treasure' Show Belongs in a Museum. SiriusXM Radio Should Release It to the Public." Steemit.com, September 2017.

"Don't Do Me Like That: Review." *Cashbox*, November 17, 1979.

Dunn, Kevin. "Long After Dark hit for Petty." *The Rocket*, January 21, 1983.

Edwards, Gavin. "Tom Petty Reunites Mudcrutch." *Rolling Stone*, May 1, 2008.

Ellis, Ralph. "Tom Petty died of accidental drug overdose, medical examiner says." CNN.com, January 20, 2018.

Farber, Jim. "On his new CD, Petty rips today's pop culture." *The Gainesville Sun*, October 9, 2002.

"Somewhere You Feel Free: Behind the Making of Tom Petty's *Wildflowers*." *The Guardian*, November 10, 2021.

Farley, Christopher John. "Music: Echo." *Time*, May 10, 1999.

Fong-Torres, Ben. "Go After What You Love." *Parade*, April 25, 2010.

Fricke, David. "It's Good To Be King." *Rolling Stone*, December 10, 2009.

"Tom Petty's Rock & Roll Refuge." *Rolling Stone,* August 14, 2014.

"Remember Tom Petty, 1950–2017." *Rolling Stone*, October 18, 2017.

Gans, David. "Tom Petty: Hot spell." *Hit Parader*, April 1983.

Gardner, Elysa. "American Boys." *Rolling Stone*, November 3, 1994.

GG. "Tom Petty & The Heartbreakers: Mojo." *Billboard*, June 12, 2010.

Giles, Jeff. "When Tom Petty and The Heartbreakers Cleared The Vaults On 'Playback.'" *Ultimate Classic Rock*, November 21, 2015.

Gilmore, Mikal. "Tom Petty's Real-Life Nightmares: Rocker on 'Damn the Torpedoes' Woes.'" *Rolling Stone*, February 21, 1980.

Goldberg, Michael. "Back on the Road: Tom Petty Teams Up with New Pal Bob Dylan." *Rolling Stone*, January 16, 1986.

Gonzales, David. "Tom Petty Goes to the Vault in Live Offering Spanning Decades." *The Epoch Times*, March 3, 2010.

Goodman, Fred. "How Tom Petty Beat the Labels." *Billboard*, October 6, 2017.

Gotz, David M. "*Record Review* Interview: Tom Petty." *Record Review*, August 1979.

"Interview: Petty Gets His Torpedoes Together and Damns Ahead To The Airwaves." *Record Review*, February 1980.

Graff, Gary. "Byrds Legend Chris Hillman Premieres Tom Petty-Produced 'Bidin' My Time.'" *Billboard*, September 19, 2017.

Greene, Andy. "Rock & Roll Daily: Tom Petty Speaks Out About the Year's Least Requested Reunion: Mudcrutch." *Rolling Stone*, December 5, 2007.

"Tom Petty on Past Confederate Flag Use: It Was Downright Stupid." *Rolling Stone*, July 14, 2015.

"Drummer Steve Ferrone on His Years With Tom Petty, George Harrison, Duran Duran, and More." *Rolling Stone*, October 21, 2020.

"In One Year & Out The Other: What Might Have Been (A Continuing Saga)." *Ampersand*, March 1981.

Hasty, Katie. "Tom Petty box set An American Treasure turns sadness to joy for bandmate Benmont Tench." *Entertainment Weekly*, September 27, 2018.

Hilburn, Robert. "Petty Courts Fans on 'Lawsuit Tour.'" *The Los Angeles Times*, July 27, 1979.

"Album Review: Petty Gets His Message Across." *The Sarasota Herald-Tribune*, November 6, 1982.

"Petty-Heartbreakers 'Let Me Up': Full Speed Ahead.'" *The Los Angeles Times*, April 19, 1987.

Hochman, Steve. "Tom Petty Griping About the Music Industry? Nah, It's Just a Metaphor." *The Los Angeles Times*, June 30, 2022.

Jackson, Blair. "Tom Petty & the Heartbreakers: It's Only Rock 'n' Roll (And That's The Point)." *Bay Area Magazine*, April 7, 1978.

"Tom Petty's Rock Victory." *Bay Area Magazine*, December 1979.

Jurgensen, John. "Rock God Or Mere Mortal?" *The Wall Street Journal*, November 20, 2009.

Kipnis, Jill. "Career Film Will Offer Anatomy of a Rock Band." *Billboard*, March 25, 2006.

Ladd, Jim. "Tom Petty and the Heartbreakers." *The Album Network*, April 16, 1999.

Latimer, David. "Get lucky with Tom Petty tribute: Newer artists reinvent old Petty tracks for new compilation." *The Paisano*, October 18, 1994.

Lenz, Toni. "Anti-nuke musings." *The Montclarion*, September 27, 1979.

Leroux, Noel. "The Day Tom Petty Met 'The King' Is the Stuff of Music Legends." *Gainesville Downtown*, October 18, 2019.

Lewis, Randy. "Review: 'The Live Anthology' by Tom Petty & the Heartbreakers." *The Los Angeles Times*, November 26, 2009.

"Tom Petty's final interview: There was supposed to have been so much more." *The Los Angeles Times*, October 13, 2017.

Lewis, Randy. "Tom Petty's death is still a hard reminder for aging rockers about the downside of life on the road." *The Los Angeles Times*, October 5, 2018.

"Tom Petty's widow and daughters reach agreement over his estate." The Los Angeles Times, December 18, 2019.

Lewry, Fraser. "Relive the historic moment Tom Petty and surprise guest Axl Rose duetted on MTV." Loudersound.com, March 8, 2022.

Marsh, Dave. "*Tom Petty and the Heartbreakers* Review." *Meriden-Southington Journal*, December 22, 1976.

"Tom Petty." *Musician*, July 1981.

Martin, Tim. "A Tribute to Tom Petty: You Got Lucky." *Round Up*, September 15, 1994.

McCormick, Neil. "Tom Petty: A rock star for the ages." *The Daily Telegraph*. June 16, 2012.

"Meet Tom Petty's 'New' Old Band." *Entertainment Weekly*, April 17, 2008.

Mettler, Mike. "Mojo Workin'." *Sound & Vision*, June–July–August 2010.

Milward, John. "Tom Petty and the Heartbreakers: Live review." *Rolling Stone*, January 26, 1978.

"More Than a Petty Face." *Melody Maker*, May 26, 1977.

Myers, Maddy. "Grand Theft Auto 6 trailer brings back a 1989 Tom Petty Song." *Polygone*, December 4, 2023.

Newcomb, Brian Q. "Tom Petty & The Heartbreakers: 40th Anniversary Tour (Concert Review)." *The Fire Note*, May 18, 2017.

Newman, Melinda. "Tom Petty: A Portrait of the Artist." *Billboard*, December 3, 2005.

"Reflections and Gratitude at Milestone Passes." *Billboard*, March 25, 2006.

O'Hare, Kevin. "From the archives: Tom Petty Interview." Masslive.com, October 2, 2017.

Olson, Cathy Applefeld. "Tom Petty Originally Wrote 'Free Fallin'' Just to Make Jeff Lynne Laugh." *Billboard*, June 6, 2016.

Palmer, Robert. "The Pop Life: Tom Petty: Ready to Fight the Good Fight." *The New York Times*, May 6, 1981.

"'Live Aid' Provided Reunions of 60's Bands." *The New York Times*, July 15, 1985.

Pareles, Jon. "Recordings View: Shake, Rattle and Growing Old With the Wilburys." *The New York Times*, November 4, 1990.

Pang, K. "Mike Judge feeling fine as 'King of the Hill' signs off." *Chicago Tribune*, August 22, 2021.

Parker, Lyndsey. "Remember Tom Petty's crazy, controversial 'Don't Come Around Here No More' music video." *Yahoo! Entertainment*, February 27, 2020.

Peeples, Stephen K. "Tom Petty and the Heartbreakers: Hogtown boys make good." *Rock Around the World*, October 1977.

Petty, Tom, and Steve Hochman. "If It's Monday, This Must Be Miami." *Rolling Stone*, October 5, 1989.

Pond, Steve. "Tom Petty battles MCA over album pricing." *Rolling Stone*, March 19, 1981.

"Tom Petty: A rock & roll hero keeps fighting on." *Rolling Stone*, July 23, 1981.

Power, Ed. "Rock: Tom Petty and the Heartbreakers, the 02, Dublin." *Irish Independent*, June 11, 2012.

Raferty, Brian. "Remembering Tom Petty." *Wired*, October 3, 2017.

Rayl, Salley. "Tom Petty files for bankruptcy." *Rolling Stone*, August 9, 1979.

Ressner, Jeffrey. "Tom Petty Goes It Alone." *Rolling Stone*, April 20, 1989.

"Tom Petty: Traveling Heartbreaker." *CD Review*, October 1991.

Roberts, Randall. "Tom Petty and the Heartbreakers, an L.A. band, stare at 'Hypnotic Eye.'" *The Los Angeles Times*, June 18, 2014.

Rodrick, Stephen." Tom Petty's Last Rolling Stone Interview." *Rolling Stone*, October 5, 2017.

Rosen, Craig. "How promotion man Jon Scott helped make Tom Petty a star." *Yahoo! Entertainment*, October 4, 2017.

Rotman, Natalie. "Petty-ness: Tom Petty releases 'Live Anthology.'" *Provo Daily Herald*, December 4, 2009.

Scaggs, Austin. "Petty's Last Summer Tour?" *Rolling Stone*, April 20, 2006.

Schager, Nick. "Review: *Runnin' Down a Dream*: Tom Petty and the Heartbreakers." *Slant*, October 13, 2007.

Schaults, Janine. "The Making of 'Mojo.'" *Chicago Tribune*, June 2, 2010.

Schlenker, Dave. "Grapevine: Tom Petty takes it home." *Gainesville Magazine*, December 2005.

Schruers, Fred. "Long After Dark." *Rolling Stone*, January 20, 1983.

"Tom Petty: The Rolling Stone Interview." *Rolling Stone*, July 8, 1999.

"This Time It's Personal." *Billboard*, July 26, 2014.

Schwab, Frank. "Tom Petty's Super Bowl XLII halftime show was classic Petty." *Y! Sports*, October 2, 2017.

Selvin, Joel. "Petty Ready to Play." *The San Francisco Chronicle*, January 9, 1997.

"They've Had Enough—Just for Now." *The San Francisco Chronicle*, February 16, 1997.

"More than Petty gripe." *The San Francisco Chronicle*, October 6, 2002.

Serpick, Evan, and Charley Rogulewski. "The Patchouli Stays in the Picture." *Rolling Stone*, June 19, 2006.

Shapiro, Susin. "The Heartbreak Kid." *Sounds*, April 9, 1977.

Simmons, Sylvie. "Rock of Ages." *Mojo*, October 2006.

Sinclair, Tom. "Tom Petty and the Heartbreakers: Greatest Hits." *Entertainment Weekly*, November 19, 1993.

Snider, Mike. "Tom Petty's live legacy gets the mega-
box-set treatment." *USA Today*, December 20, 2009.

Strauss, Neil. "Tom Petty's Last Dance." *Rolling Stone*, July 13, 2006.

Streeter, Leslie. "Tom Petty in Gainesville: A Heartbreaker Comes Home." *The Palm Beach Post*, September 22, 2006.

Sullivan, Jim. "Warren Zanes Tells The Lesser Known Story Of Tom Petty's Life In New Biography." WBUR.org, November 10, 2015.

Swartley, Ariel. "Full speed ahead for Tom Petty." *Rolling Stone*, December 13, 1979.

Taylor, Jonathon. "Bob Dylan Plus Tom Petty Adds Up To Tour De Force for Concert." *Chicago Tribute*, June 15, 1986.

Thompson, Art. "Heartbreaker Hideout: In The Studio With Tom Petty & Mike Campbell." *Guitar Player*, May 1999.

"30 Years & Counting." *Guitar Player*, July 2006. "Recommended LPs: Pop." *Billboard*, December
4, 1976.

"Tom Petty Defendant in 2 Court Actions." *Billboard*, June 9, 1979.

"Tom Petty Picks Elvis Presley Songs That Influenced His Music." *Rolling Stone*, October 27, 2011.

"Tom Petty & the Heartbreakers, 'Mojo.'" *Billboard*, June 4, 2010.

"Tom Petty Tribute Album Is One Tribute Worth Listening To." *The Stony Brook Statesman*, October 24, 1994.

"Tom Petty's 50 Greatest Songs." *Rolling Stone*, November 28, 2020.

"Tom Petty's Pet Sounds." *Newsweek*, November 7, 1994.

Uhelszki, Jaan. "Tom Petty: Anatomy of Rockstar." *Harp*, July 25, 2006.

Wild, David. "Rock & Roll: Petty, Aim, Fire!" *Rolling Stone*, March 28, 2002.

"The Ten Things That Piss Off Tom Petty." *Rolling Stone*, November 14, 2002.

Williams, Stereo. "Tom Petty's Remarkable Stand Against the Confederate Flag." *Daily Beast*, October 7, 2017.

Willman, Chris. "Petty Laughs Last on 'Full Moon Fever.'" *The Los Angeles Times*, April 23, 1989.

"The Great Wide Open." *M: Music & Musicians*, September–October 2010.

"Concert Review: Tom Petty Wraps Up Retrospective Tour With Galvanizing Hollywood Bowl Stand." *Variety*, September 23, 2017.

"Tom Petty's Bandmates Tell Stories Behind Lost Tracks at 'American Treasure' Preview Event." *Variety*, August 25, 2018.

"How Tom Petty's 'She's the One' Became

an 'Angel Dream' Come True: Mike Campbell and Ryan Ulyate on a 25th Anniversary Revamp." *Variety*, July 10, 2021.

Wiser, Carl. "Mike Campbell." *Songfacts*, November 13, 2003.

Wolens, Joshua. "Spotify registers ridiculous increase in Tom Petty streams as GTA6 trailer drives everyone dad rock mad." *PC Gamer*, December 6, 2023.

Zanes, Warren. "Tom Petty Was Rock 'n' Roll's Ambassador to the World." *Slate*, October 3, 2017.

Zollo, Paul. "Tom Petty on Bob Dylan." *American Songwriter*, August 2, 2020. Hillman, Chris. *Time*

BOOKS

Between: My Life as Byrd, Burrito Brother, and Beyond. New York: BMG Books, 2020.

Howe, Zoe. *Stevie Nicks: Visions, Dreams & Rumours*. New York: Overlook Omnibus, 2015.

James, Richard. *On Track . . . Tom Petty: Every Album, Every Song*. Tewkesbury, UK: Sonicbond Publishing, 2021.

Kealing, Bob. *Good Day Sunshine State: How The Beatles Rocked Florida*. Gainesville, Florida: University Press of Florida, 2023.

Marks, Craig, and Rob Tannenbaum. *I Want My MTV: The Uncensored Story of the Music Video Revolution*. New York: Dutton, 2011.

McKittrick, Christopher. *Somewhere You Feel Free: Tom Petty and Los Angeles*. New York: Post Hill Press, 2020.

Mehr, Bob. *Trouble Boys: The True Story of The Replacements*. Boston: Da Capo Press, 2016.

Scott, Jon. *Tom Petty and Me: My Rock 'n' Roll Adventures with Tom Petty*. Sherman Oaks, CA:
CB Publishing, 2018.

Stewart, Dave. *Sweet Dreams Are Made of This: A Life in Music*. New York: New American Library, 2016.

Whitburn, Joel. *Joel Whitburn's Top Pop Albums 1966–2016*. Menomonee Falls, WI: Record Research Inc., 2018.

Joe Whitburn Presents Top Pop Singles Vol. 1: 1955–1989. Menomonee Falls, WI: Record Research Inc., 2021.

Joe Whitburn Presents Top Pop Singles Vol. 2: 1990–2022. Menomonee Falls, WI: Record Research Inc., 2023.

Zanes, Warren. *Petty: The Biography*. New York: St. Martin's Griffin, 2016.

Zollo, Paul. *Conversations With Tom Petty: Expanded Edition*. New York: Omnibus Press, 2005.

OTHER

Paul Zollo interview. "As It Happens," CBC Radio, October 3, 2017.

"Tom Petty's daughter opens up about making
'An American Treasure.'" *CBS This Morning*, October 2, 2018.

Tom Petty: The Ultimate Guide to His Music & Legend. *Rolling Stone* Special Tribute Edition, 2017.

WEBSITES

thepettyarchives.com

thepttv.net

tompetty.com

wikipedia.org

x.com

youtube.com

ztribe.com

A note on charts: All chart placings are from *Billboard*—the *Billboard* 200, the main albums chart, and the Hot 100, the main singles chart.
The magazine also has numerous other charts for tracks released both as official singles or only provided to radio stations for airplay. The Mainstream Rock Tracks chart is the one that's been the most prominent in Tom Petty's career; though the chart has gone under different names over the years, it is referred to the "Mainstream Rock Tracks" chart throughout this book for the sake of simplicity.

ABOUT THE AUTHOR

Gillian G. Gaar is the author of numerous books, including She's a Rebel: The History of Women in Rock & Roll, Entertain Us: The Rise of Nirvana, Return of the King: Elvis Presley's Great Comeback, World Domination: The Sub Pop Records Story, Elton John @ 75, and Bruce Springsteen @ 75. She has written for a variety of publications and websites, including Rolling Stone, Mojo, Q, Goldmine, American Songwriter, and No Depression, in addition to being a senior editor at legendary Seattle music magazine The Rocket. She lives in Seattle.

IMAGE CREDITS

A = all, B = bottom, C = center, L = left, M = main, R = right, T = top

Alamy Stock Photos: 10 (ZUMA Press Inc.), 11R (Chronicle), 13T (United Artists), 15M, 22 (mpiRR/MediaPunch Inc.), 23R (Vinyls), 42 (Arthur D'Ammario III), 47R (Vinyls), 48 (Scott Weiner/MediaPunch Inc.), 57BL (Scott Weiner/MediaPunch Inc.), 57TR (Vinyls), 59M (kpa), 75M (Gary Gershoff/MediaPunch Inc.), 80 (Ross Marino/MediaPunch Inc.), 82 (Ross Marino/Rock Negatives/MediaPunch Inc.), 87B (AJ Pics), 89 (Pictorial Press Ltd.), 91C (IMusic), 102 (dpa picture alliance), 105 (ilpo musto), 109L (Rob Watkins), 109R (Edd Westmacott), 117 (RBM Vintage Images), 118 (Everett Collection), 123 (Jeff Moore/ZUMA Wire/Alamy Live News), 127 (Scott Weiner/MediaPunch Inc.), 128T (Stephen Dorian Miner/Mediapunch Inc.), 129TL (Stephen Dorian Miner/Mediapunch Inc.), 131 (Tsuni/USA), 135B (Andre Jenny), 136M and 137BL (Chris McKay/MediaPunch Inc.), 144 (Hoo-Me/Storms Media Group), 146 (Chris McKay/MediaPunch Inc.), 147T (Tina Fultz/ZUMA Press), 147B (Chris McKay/MediaPunch Inc.), 148M (©Kevin Estrada/MediaPunch), 149 (Jerry Holt/*Minneapolis Star Tribune*/TNS/Alamy Live News), 151 (©Kevin Estrada/MediaPunch), 152 (Tammie Arroyo/AFF), 154–155A (© Jerome Brunet/ZUMA Press), 161 (© Hector Acevedo/ZUMApress.com), 164 and 165M (WENN Rights Ltd.), 166 (ZUMA Press), 167B (Rockstar Photography), 170 (WENN Rights Ltd.), 177 (Bobby Singh), 190-191 (Bobby Singh). **Robert Alford:** 72, 158, 178. **Associated Press:** 106 (Bebeto Matthews), 120 (©Kevin Estrada/MediaPunch/IPx), 121M (©Kevin Estrada/Media-Punch/IPx), 135T (Ed Betz), 153T (A-PIZZELLO), 157 (Matt Slocum), 173M (Chris Pizzello/Invision), 175 (Amy Harris/Invision). **Avalon:** 7 (LFI), 67 (Denis O'Regan). **Getty Images:** 2 (Michael Ochs Archives), 4 (Aaron Rapoport/Corbis Historical), 8 (Richard E. Aaron/Redferns), 16 (Jim McCrary/Redferns), 18 and 19 (Jim McCrary/Redferns), 20 (Richard E. Aaron/Redferns), 21 (Michael Ochs Archives), 25M (Richard E. Aaron/Redferns), 26 (Chris Walter/WireImage), 27M (Ian Dickson/Redferns), 28 (Gus Stewart/Redferns), 29 (Estate of Keith Morris/Redferns), 30 (Gus Stewart/Redferns), 31T (Ian Dickson/Redferns), 32T (Aaron Rapoport/Corbis Historical), 35M (*Los Angeles Times*), 36 (*Los Angeles Times*), 39 (Aaron Rapoport/Corbis Historical), 40 (Lynn Goldsmith/Corbis Historical), 41R (Lynn Goldsmith/Corbis Historical), 43TL (Chris Walter), 44M (Paul Natkin), 47M (Gary Gershoff), 50–51 (Virginia Turbett/Redferns), 53M (Aaron Rapoport/Corbis Historical), 54 (George Rose/Hulton Archive), 55TL (Lynn Goldsmith/Corbis Historical), 56 (Larry Hulst/Michael Ochs Archive), 60 (Chris Walter/WireImage), 61T (Lynn Goldsmith/Corbis Historical), 62–63 (Bertrand Laforet/Gamma-Rapho), 65 (Aaron Rapoport/Corbis Historical), 68 (Paul Natkin), 73B (Deborah Feingold/Corbis Premium Historical), 77–77 (Koh Hasebe/Shinko Music/Hulton Archive), 79 (Aaron Rapoport/Corbis Historical), 81M (Aaron Rapoport/Corbis Historical), 83TR (Aaron Rapoport/Corbis Historical), 91T (Dave Hogan/Hulton Archive), 92 (Harry Borden), 93BL (Rick Eglinton/*Toronto Star*), 94–95 (Jeffrey Mayer/WireImage), 97TL (Aaron Rapoport/Corbis Historical), 99M (Aaron Rapoport/Corbis Historical), 100T (Aaron Rapoport/Corbis Historical), 104 (Lynn Goldsmith/Corbis Historical), 109C (Al Schaben/*Los Angeles Times*), 111L (Al Pereira/Michael Ochs Archives), 115M (Jim Steinfeldt/Michael Ochs Archives), 116 (Jim Steinfeldt/Michael Ochs Archives), 119M (Rick Diamond/Archive Photos), 124 (Karl Mondon/MediaNews Group/*The Mercury News*), 125 (Liz Hafalia/*The San Francisco Chronicle*), 134 (KMazur/WireImage), 138 and 139T (Frazer Harrison), 140 and 141T (KMazur/WireImage), 163 (Chris Ryan/Corbis), 169 (Aaron Rapoport/Corbis Historical), 172 (Scott Dudelson), 181 (Aaron Rapoport/Corbis Historical), 183 (Rick Eglinton/*Toronto Star*). **Photofest:** 86, 87T. **Quarto:** 11L, 17, 41L, 71R, 88L, 88R, 90, 108. **Shutterstock:** 132 and 133T (©Berliner Studio/BEImages). **UrbanImage.tv:** 24 (Adrian Boot), 112 (Adrian Boot), 143 (Adrian Boot). **Frank White Photo Agency:** 70 (Dean Messina), 71T (Dean Messina), 85 (John T. Comerford).

INDEX

To Danielle and Lee Bacon
Keep pursuing your dreams!

Quarto.com

First Published in 2025 by Motorbooks, an imprint of The Quarto Group,
100 Cummings Center, Suite 265-D, Beverly, MA 01915, USA.
T (978) 282-9590 F (978) 283-2742

EEA Representation, WTS Tax d.o.o.,
Žanova ulica 3, 4000 Kranj, Slovenia.
www.wts-tax.si

29 28 27 26 25   1 2 3 4 5

ISBN: 978-0-7603-9261-4

Digital edition published in 2025
eISBN: 978-0-7603-9262-1

Library of Congress Cataloging-in-Publication Data

Names: Gaar, Gillian G., 1959- author.
Title: Tom Petty : the life & music / Gillian G. Gaar.
Description: Beverly, MA : Motorbooks, 2025. | Includes bibliographical references and index. | Summary: "A unique and lavishly produced celebration of the iconic rocker, Tom Petty: The Life & Music examines an extraordinary career through the lens of 75 key events and releases"-- Provided by publisher.
Identifiers: LCCN 2025003019 | ISBN 9780760392614 | ISBN 9780760392621 (ebook)
Subjects: LCSH: Petty, Tom. | Heartbreakers (Musical group) | Rock musicians--United States--Biography.
Classification: LCC ML410.P3135 G23 2025 | DDC 782.42166092 [B]--dc23/eng/20250122
LC record available at https://lccn.loc.gov/2025003019

Design: www.traffic-design.co.uk
Slipcase Image: Estate of Keith Morris/Redferns/Getty Images
Book Cover Image: ZUMA Press, Inc./Alamy Stock Photo

Printed in China